# NAVIGATING

# THE MINEFIELD

A Man's Guide

to Successful Internet Dating

Philip Ford

Copyright © Philip Ford 2021
This book is sold subject to the condition that it shall not, by way of trade or otherwise, be lent, resold, hired out, or otherwise circulated without the publisher's prior consent in any form of binding or cover other than that in which it is published and without a similar condition including this condition being imposed on the subsequent publisher.
The moral right of Philip Ford has been asserted.
ISBN-13: 9798542403014

To Alice Emma. You are my gift to the world!

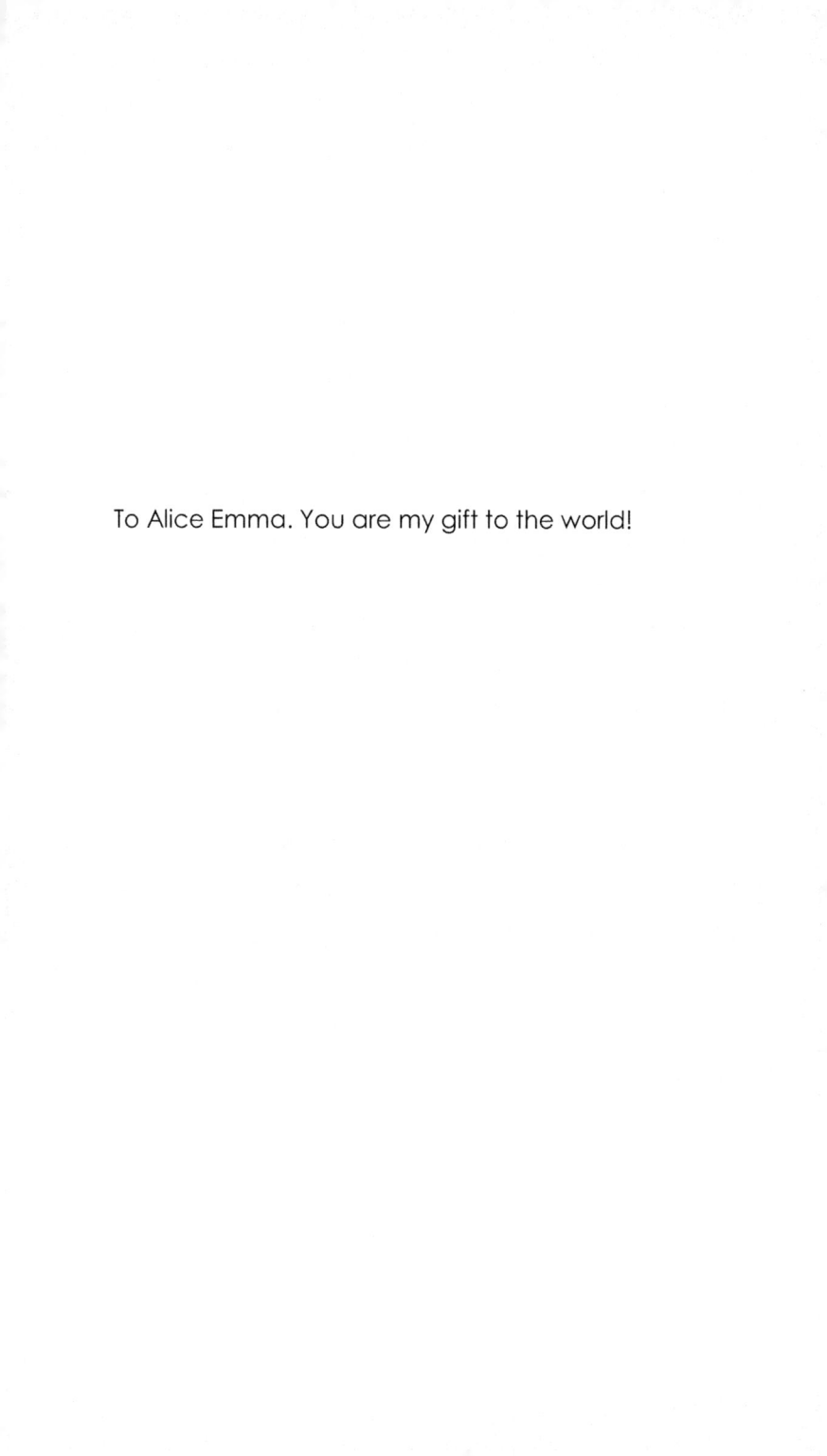

# CONTENTS

INTRODUCTION ............................................................................ 1
CHAPTER 1 Breaking the stigma .............................................. 3
CHAPTER 2 Before we begin ..................................................... 8
CHAPTER 3 Creating your profile ........................................... 22
CHAPTER 4 Finding someone and sending the first message ................................................................................... 35
CHAPTER 5 You've got mail .................................................... 47
CHAPTER 6 Making a date ..................................................... 73
CHAPTER 7 After the date ..................................................... 120
CHAPTER 8 Your second date and more ........................... 129
CHAPTER 9 The silly little mistakes ......................................... 145
IN CONCLUSION .................................................................... 177
ABOUT THE AUTHOR ............................................................. 180

# INTRODUCTION

In 1994 kiss.com became the first ever dating website followed by match.com in 1995. A year later in 1996 Yahoo listed 16 dating websites. As of 2020 there are over 1,400 dating websites available in the UK. After twenty plus years you'd think we would have it mastered. Yet to this day online dating remains a strange, confusing and frightening place to most.

*"It is not the strongest of the species that survives, not the most intelligent that survives. It is the one that is most adaptable to change."* – Charles Darwin (maybe)

In 2010 I entered the world of online dating as a socially awkward guy who'd never had much success with women. I had some high's, I had some lows. I certainly was not the strongest or most intelligent, I was however able to adapt, change and learn as I went. In 2015 I met the woman who would become my wife. In 2020 a friend suggested I write this book after advice given from my own experience proved invaluable to him.

I need to state from the get-go, I am not a player or a pick up artist. I have no magic system to make women want to sleep with you. If that's what you are looking for you will not find it here. There are plenty of authors out there making those promises, I suggest you seek one of them and good luck. I am not writing this as a guide to pick up and sleep with hundreds of women, if anything consider this more of a guide on how not to be an arsehole.

# CHAPTER 1

# Breaking the stigma

Whether you're brand new or you've been here before there is a stigma attached to online dating. I know I avoided it for a long time on the belief it was for creeps and losers who couldn't meet women in real life. What would online dating say about me? I was wrong and getting over that stigma was life changing for me. Before you can expect any kind of success you also need to make sure you do not have the same stigma. Because you cannot approach anything with negativity and expect anything other than negativity in return.

We work online, shop online, do our banking and upload our entire lives onto social media. Why shouldn't you look for love online? Think of every way the internet has made your life better or easier, why should online dating be any different? Why would you want to limit yourself? Why wouldn't you want to make yourself available to a much larger market? Why wouldn't you want to see everyone who's available out there? Once you get over the stigma attached to online dating you will realise the potential and all the possibilities that lay before you.

Online dating is for everyone! Well everyone over eighteen at least. It doesn't take more than ten seconds to do a Google search and realise just how wide the market is. If you won't date outside of your religion there's a website for you. If you wear a uniform there is a dating website just for you. If you want to have affairs with married people there's a website for you. Love classical music there's a website for you. If you want to meet rural and countryside people there's a website for you. If you'll only date millionaire's and CEO's there is a website just for you, the list goes on.

So whatever stigma's or hesitation's you may have, put them aside. You are not too old, or overweight, or ugly, or out of touch, there is a whole new world out there waiting for you to discover it. You don't even need to get off your sofa. At least not to begin with.

Let me address some of these obvious concerns.

- You're too old. Incorrect! When I started internet dating I was 24, my boss at work was on the same sites as me, he was 47. He was easily getting 10 times the amount of interest I was. As you get older your target audience becomes more realistic. In my 20's most women of a similar age expected a man to make a six-figure salary, have a big house and a flash car. However at his age, if you were employed, still had all your own teeth and didn't live in a bed sit you were a winner!

- You think you're too overweight or ugly. Believe it or not physical appearance is not the be all and end all for women. We are the more visual of the two sexes. The majority of women don't want a man who is more attractive than they are. Washing daily, brushing your teeth, combing your hair and dressing well generally counts for more, and weight can always be lost.

- You're too out of touch. Look at it from a different perspective your interests are unique and eccentric. Trust me there is someone out there for you. You're not out of touch, You're just not mainstream.

- You won't find anyone decent online. Well as of 2019 93% of households in the UK had internet access. Over 15 million people in the UK have registered for online dating. One in five relationships now starts online. It may seem strange to you but you can't stop progress. This is the way were moving forward. The fact is if you were succeeding elsewhere you wouldn't even be considering it. You definitely wouldn't be reading this so don't believe it because it's just not true.

- It's a scam. Again untrue, well mostly untrue. Yes some sites and apps are better than others. Some have extortionate fees, some are free. I'm not going to recommend which to use and which to avoid. I haven't used all of them and I want to remain unbiased. Also they're not paying me shit so why would I? Google is your friend though and will help you figure it out. Some sites may make promises like "Love guaranteed" or "unique profiling and matching personality software." The simple fact is you'll get out what you put in. Just like real life. Want to find someone? You need to go and find them! No website, AI or match-making software is going to do everything for you. As for people trying to scam you. Well they do exist just as they do in the real world. There are fake profiles, and people who will rinse you for everything you have given half the chance. Let your common sense guide you. Don't give strangers money or your bank details. Also if a gorgeous 21-year-old messages you out of the blue wanting to meet in the woods for hot sex, the odds are it's a set-up, you're getting beaten up and robbed. Over all though there are plenty of legitimate people out there and this is a great way to meet them.

By joining a dating website you will instantly met with a selection of people who are there because they are actively looking to meet someone. Think about that, it's already done half the job for you. I used to see a girl in a bar on a night out and I'd think, "what if she doesn't want to be disturbed? What if she has a boyfriend?" Plus one hundred other thoughts and reasons not to go and talk to her. A dating website removes that problem, they are openly saying I am available and I am looking. Now you may not be what they are looking for but I said it has done half the job for you not all of it.

# CHAPTER 2

# Before we begin

So you've decided to take the plunge and put yourself on the market, congratulations. Before you start you need to sit down and be very honest with yourself. Decide exactly what it is you want out of this, what is acceptable for you and what is not. As well as what you bring to the table. Think of it like a business meeting, you wouldn't walk into a business deal and succeed in getting what you want without having done your research first and this is no different. So sit down with a pen and paper and work out honestly what you want.

So are you looking to date and meet new people? Are you looking to find the one? Maybe you just want to hook up and have no strings attached sex. There is no shame in any of the answers but you need to be honest with yourself about what exactly you are looking for before you start. So in turn you can be honest with the people you interact with and who you're trying to attract. There is no sense in wasting your time or theirs. Also note there are plenty of jaded, bitter and broken people out there. Men and women. A lot of them are this way because they were misled and lied to. You don't need to add to these people! The world is a harsh enough place as it is. If that didn't make sense to you what I'm saying is if you just want casual sex be honest don't mislead someone and hurt them further down the road. On the flip side if you want a lasting relationship don't look for someone who wants the opposite and then end up hurt yourself. Like I said in my introduction consider this a guide on how not to be an arsehole.

So take your pen and paper and work out exactly what you want, casual/dating/relationship, the Queen to the New World Order you'll create from the ashes of society. Whatever but be honest.

Next work out what's important to you. This is the part where you may feel like a horrible person but there is no sense in lying to yourself it will only lead to hurt later, for you and others if you don't. If you're a vegan for example and it is incredibly important that you only date another vegan write that down and do not compromise, otherwise you are just setting yourself up for failure. If you're a non-smoker and hate smoking, that is important to you do not compromise. If you are shallow and will only date people who are a physical 10. (I'd suggest you readjust your values) But if that's important, write it down and don't compromise.

Next figure out what you bring to the table and write it down. What positive attributes do you have and why should people want them? It is important you know your self-worth because if you don't others won't either. It is also important to consider if you want to have high standards in what you expect from a partner why should they be any different in what they expect from you in return? Know your self-worth and do not settle for less. You should not expect a prospective partner to do any different for you.

If you're unsure let me give you an example of what my last piece of paper looked like.

I am looking to date and meet new people with the possibility of it leading to a relationship if and when I meet the right person.

It is important to me that they understand that my job is more than a job to me it is my passion and a way of life, not just a pay check (a lot of people could not accept this, that was cool I wished them all the best and moved on).

I am active and like to spend my time outdoors. I want someone who is also active and enjoys nature, being outside, hiking etc. If someone cannot enjoy the countryside with me we probably won't spend any quality time together. (this is important to me I want someone who will hike, wild swim and camp with me)

I love animals I have pets (This is important to me anyone who cannot accept this is not the one for me).

I do not want someone who is naturally devious or manipulative. If we fall out I expect my other half to be able to communicate her problems with me honestly so we can resolve them maturely. I don't want to give my time to someone who will play mind games, if I've pissed her off (In the past I've had girlfriends with a phone book full of desperate men who she will suddenly contact in an attempt to make me jealous if we annoy one another). I don't have any tolerance for someone who can't resolve problems like an adult and will resort to things like this.

I will not date someone who leads an active criminal lifestyle. I have too much to lose by being associated with someone as such (This is important to me and I will not compromise).

Religious views are unimportant to me, I will date anyone of any religion and I will respect their belief's however I will not convert or change my beliefs for anyone (this meant it did not work out between me and some people, I wished them all the best and moved on).

Vegetarianism, veganism is not a problem for me, I'll respect your lifestyle I'm happy to eat vegan or vegetarian food occasionally and learn new recipes. However I am unwilling to change my lifestyle and stop eating meat completely (this was a problem for some people I wished them all the best and moved on).

Hair colour, eye colour, height, breast size complexion is unimportant to me as long as they look after themselves. Self-worth, confidence and humour are more important to me.

What I bring to the table. I am employed and incredibly passionate about it. I have a car, I am a homeowner. I lead an active lifestyle spending as much time as I can outdoors, I love nature, I like to explore, I like history and historical places. I'm well-travelled. I have a warped sense of humour (it's a positive for some). My plus points may be negative for others I accept we cannot all get along, that is the way of the world.

Once you have worked out what you want and what you offer in return, things should fall into place. A simple comparison from a man's point of view is when you want to buy a new car (please note I am not comparing women to cars, no, no cars are much easier to deal with). When you know exactly what car you want, what you require you won't waste your time looking at what you don't want. You don't test drive something you have zero intention of buying, do you?

## A point on self-worth

I'm writing this paragraph from my own personal experience, some of you may relate some will not. In many aspects of my life I know my self-worth and I am extremely confident. However around women was not one of these places. I was unable to see what a woman would see in me. Years later I still struggle with this from time to time. All I can tell you is DO NOT think about that. You need to know your worth to YOURSELF! Hint is in the word, self-worth. When you have that others will see it in you. This is also known as confidence, and confidence for most of us is the most desirable thing we will ever bring to the table.

A final point on self-worth. Having self-worth and knowing what you want is a good thing. But there is a fine line between that and arrogance. Do not get the two mixed up. Confidence is attractive, rudeness, arrogance and thinking you're better than others is not. To quote Rocky Balboa, "If you know what you're worth then go and get what you're worth!" That is the point I am making, I AM NOT telling you it is OK to treat others badly or look down on them. Remember don't be an arsehole.

Let me give you a real example that happened to me. In 2013 I dated a PA she had a highly paid job with a clear career path. I had my (lower paid) dream job with 100% job satisfaction. I didn't think the salary gap was important. Evidently it was to her. At first it was fun and exciting, as it should be, but it didn't work. She used to say things I'll never forget like, "I drive a brand-new Audi where as you think it's OK to drive a 15-year-old Ford."

Her success and ambition gave her confidence I found that attractive, the arrogance and elitism making her believe I was beneath her made her ugly. Now you may think why should she settle for someone who earns less or wasn't as career driven as her? After all didn't she just know her self-worth? The answer is yes of course. She shouldn't settle if that is important to her! But it is worth noting it was her attitude that made me leave her, not her leave me. Because I also knew my self-worth enough to know I was worth more than the way she saw and treated me. When it happened she couldn't understand how someone like me could leave someone like her. Again arrogant and unattractive even to someone "beneath her". – Don't be like that.

## Identifying your flaws and short comings

Before you start this is something you should also do. Please note you are doing this for you no one else! I know I didn't the first time round and it's something I wish I had done. I learnt my lesson after that and I always did before entering the dating scene, because I preferred to rectify things myself rather than have them pointed out or put off my dates. Single men get complacent, men who have just got out of long-term relationships have developed bad habits. Were all guilty of this in one way or another. I'm not talking about uphauling your life, more like polishing the rough edges. So take a look at yourself and think where have you let things go? When dating you want to put the best version of you forwards. This again ties in with self-worth making these little fixes in your life will make you feel better which in turn will make you project a better you.

For example, the last time I entered the online dating world I had just ended a two-year relationship and I had found myself in a rut. I was moving like a sloth, generally feeling sorry for myself, not doing the things I loved and spending all my time slouched on the couch. I didn't like myself, and I knew if I didn't like myself why should anyone else? Things had to change. So I changed things I set a bed time to stop me sleeping till noon. As soon as I woke up I forced myself to get into the shower, shave, brush my teeth and put on nice clothes suitable for going outside. Even if I had no plans to go outside. Instead of putting on my dressing gown going downstairs and flopping on the couch. I cleaned my entire house, mowed the lawn, swept the patio, cleaned my car inside and out. Cleaned out my fridge, threw out the take away menu's went to the shops and bought vegetables. I didn't even look at registering myself on a dating site until I was happy I resembled a human once again.

So look at the little things, and pay attention to the fine details. Are your shoes falling apart? Have you bought new clothes in the last decade? When was the last time you had a haircut? When did you last see a dentist or hygienist? Do you know what deodorant is? Does that swastika tattoo need covering up? Have you ever been to a GUM clinic, do you have reason to think you should go?

The first date I ever had, I remember as I was getting dressed to go out. It dawned on me I couldn't remember the last time I bought new underwear. I stood there looking at myself thinking you won't get lucky in these. The next day I took myself shopping. Another time as I got in my car to go meet someone I realised the inside of it had its own eco system. This would not do if I was going to be picking her up on future dates. So the next day I cleaned it inside and out then kept it clean. Little things like this can make all the difference. If you're not giving yourself the best you can you are not going to give it or get it from anyone else.

To hammer the point home on this you are doing this for you to be the best version of yourself not to impress women. This is not a fake it until you make it situation. These little fixes are for you and they're permanent. It's something you need to embrace in all aspects of life not just for meeting women. It's not a temporary patch job or a stop gap allowing you to fall into bad habits a few months later. I'm married now, I still live by the rules I set and I still see the difference every day. For example, every time I go food shopping I'm dressed well, my shoulders are back and my head is up. I notice women looking at me. They then usually look back at their significant other in his worn out tracksuit with messy hair and sigh. It's not that they're wishing they were with me instead, it's just that while I'm still putting the best version of myself forwards, these women's partners stopped some time ago and have fallen into lazy bad habits. This is a double-edged sword of course. It's nice to notice you're being noticed, it keeps your confidence up, it keeps your head held high. These are all things that make you more attractive to the women you'll be meeting.

## Should you stay single for some time first?

A final thing to consider is should you be doing this? Well let me rephrase that, should you be doing this at this very moment? This lines up with improving yourself, polishing the rough edges and being the best version of yourself you can be. Ask yourself do you need to spend some time alone first? The fact is most people don't want to admit it if they do, so please be honest with yourself. Throughout my life I've met many people who just cannot be alone. They literally go from one relationship to the next. Some of them are literally living their lives in a constant state of rebound. This means they repeat the same mistakes time and time again, because they never take any time to heal, identify issues or work on them. They are almost always doomed to fail. The sad thing is these people are also some of the unhappiest people I've ever met, because their self-worth and the value they place in themselves ties directly into having someone else in their life. This is the harsh truth of the matter. No one else can truly make you happy, no one else is going to fix you. Only you can do that. If you're not enough on your own, you won't be with someone else either.

*"A gold medal is a wonderful thing. But if you're not*

*enough without it, you'll never be enough with it."* – Irv Blitzer (John Candy) *Cool Runnings*.

## In Conclusion

Before you begin you must know who you are. You need to know your strengths, weaknesses, likes, dislikes, goals, priorities and mission in life. You need to know what standards you have as well as your principles and core values. You need to know who you are and what you're about in order to attract someone possessing the same qualities you have or desire in a partner.

A strong man with strong beliefs, core values and principles will not compromise them for anyone. Believe it or not this is actually a very attractive quality in a man and it will attract the right kind of woman. This man knows what he is worth. He will not accept the wrong kind of people into his life. A man with no core values or principles will accept anyone into his life along with whatever negativity they bring with them. This never leads to anything good.

Let me give you another real-life example. Earlier I said I will not associate with anyone who lives or leads an active criminal lifestyle. In my early twenties I had a girlfriend who had successfully hidden a cocaine addiction from me for several months. When I discovered the truth I should have walked there and then. But I was young and at the time I was weak. I compromised my own principles and I stayed with her despite our core values clearly not lining up. Soon enough I found myself hanging around and associating with less than desirable people because of the new friends she was making. I found myself in places I didn't want to be, at parties I didn't want to go to, with people I didn't want to be with. For those of you that don't know, cocaine isn't cheap, the debts started mounting up. Soon I was going to find myself in a position where I'd have to help her cover those debts or deal with the people she had made them with (FUCK THAT!) As I watched her life take a nose dive eventually I saw sense. She was not the one for me I was definitely not the one for her. Not only was I making myself uncomfortable by compromising my principles for her I was now potentially putting myself at risk and not just from the dealers she owed money to. My job at the time required a spotless criminal record. Checks were carried out every twelve months I was risking everything just by being in her company.

*"Those who stand for nothing fall for everything."* – Alexander Hamilton.

Of course, no one is likely to admit to being a drug addict or an active criminal on their dating profile. Some things that don't line up with your core values and principles will be easy to identify like the things I pointed out earlier. Vegan, non-smoker etc. Others will not, that is why you need to know yourself and remain uncompromising. So should you find yourself in a similar position to me when I was younger you'll be strong enough to walk away if your principles have been compromised. Not make an exception just because you've already invested time into her and the relationship.

# CHAPTER 3

# Creating your profile

Whatever dating site you have chosen you will now be faced with several boxes to fill in. The pen and paper exercise if you did it should assist you here. Remember, be honest because the truth always comes out in the end. I want to help you fill out a few key points, the rest I will leave up to you because at the end of the day it is your unique individuality that is important.

### The profile picture (and other pictures)

This is the key point. It is the first thing anyone see's. Let's be blunt here the profile picture is the deciding factor. We are visual creatures and we need to like what we see! More so for men than women I am sure. But if we do not please the eye do not expect things to go any further.

No fake photo's! Seriously this is a common problem

and I don't know how anyone thinks they will get away with it? Maybe guys think I'll lure her in with a photo of someone else get her to fall for me then when we meet in real life it won't matter because she will have got to know the real me on the inside? The answer is NO! She will feel betrayed, lied to and very fucked off! DON'T DO IT!

No mirror selfies! It suggests vanity and implies you live such an uninteresting life no one has ever taken a decent real picture of you. No shirt off photo's, I don't care if you're competing in Mr Universe again it suggests vanity. A shirtless photo of you on holiday at the beach is acceptable but maybe not as the main profile picture. Add it to the other photo's on your profile. No old cat-fishing photo's. The best photo ever taken of me was in 2010 at sunset in New Zealand it was my dating profile photo for a long time. I could not use it today because while you can tell it is me in the photo I am a decade older. It is unrealistic.

Photos of you shitfaced with the lads in a bar are unappealing.

Photos of you with another girl, it doesn't matter if it's your sister it's a no!

Photos of your car or motorbike, no one's looking to date a transformer. So what if you have an expensive car? It implies you're superficial or materialistic. Or trying to attract a gold digger.

No group photo's. No woman wants to play guess who. They'll also make the assumption that you're the least attractive one in the group.

The you and your dog photo. Now if you have a dog why shouldn't you include a photo of the two of you? After all your dog is a huge part of your life. However it is a trend that is fast becoming old. Lots of men take photos with their dog hoping to use its cuteness to lure in women. So women may look at a photo of you and your dog and think, "Urgh another one of those." If you want to put up a you and a dog photo there are two rules to follow.

1.) Only do it if it is your dog, don't borrow your mates dog for a photo.

2.) A photo of you and your dog, not every photo of you and your dog.

To the keen fishermen out there, a photo of you holding your prize mirror carp is also not appealing. Most women will be fine with you enjoying fishing but that photo will not attract them to you.

Try to find a genuine photo of yourself taken by someone else at a time when you were happy. If you can't find a photo like that I suggest you go out and live more. You need to be interesting!

## The about me description box

Every site has this in some form or another. Don't ignore it, fill it out. How do you expect anyone to take you seriously as a potential suitor if you cannot bother to take a few minutes to fill out the description? Be honest. Like I said the truth always comes out and trying to attract the wrong sort of person will only lead to tears for you both in the end. Don't fill in your life story. When you get a date you need something to talk about after all, a bit of mystery is good.

The main thing to note about filling in the about me is in the title. It's about you. You want to write a description of yourself, what you like and what you are like. Keep it about you don't do things like list the requirements you expect to date you, or the attributes of your ideal woman. The description is for a woman to find out about you, not find out what you expect them to be. The aim is to sell yourself, make yourself appealing, not put people off (even if what you've described matches someone perfectly, the fact you've listed it will likely be a turn off). Try to appear light hearted and fun. Nothing too serious. Bear in mind when you message a woman they will look at your profile before deciding if it's worth replying to you. So how you come across is important you need to put the best version of yourself forward. Happy, funny, positive and loving life goes a lot further than reading a required check list to see if you qualify to return a message.

I know this sounds like a contradiction to what I said in Chapter two about knowing what you want, what you'll accept and what you won't, so let me simplify it. As a man you will send the vast majority of first messages. You'll be largely responsible for first contact. So you should be selecting who you message appropriately. nullifying any need or reason at all to write such lists.

From another perspective let's use the vegan example again. You've stated in your profile that you're vegan and you've messaged another vegan. She looks at your profile see's you are also vegan, thinks great and messages you back. Or she looks at your profile and see's something like, "I'm vegan, meat is murder and I won't have anything to do with anyone who disagrees or isn't vegan so don't even bother." There is a chance she may agree and message you back there is also a chance you've come across very negative, she now thinks you're a rude arsehole and doesn't message you back. trust me don't do it.

## Some things are better left unsaid

You need to choose your words carefully. What sounds better to you? Newly single looking to meet someone to go on adventures with, or I'm here because I caught my bitch ex-wife fucking our accountant. If you are reading this book because you have indeed caught your wife bedding the accountant, you have my sympathies. But seriously don't bring it up, it is not a selling point. Under no circumstances mention ex's or previous relationships in your bio.

Children, if you have them. If you have kids do not lie and say you don't. By all means confirm you have children. It is a huge part of your life and people have the right to know if they are going to become involved with you. But again choose your words carefully. I have a daughter or I have two kids reads a lot better than an in-depth bio about how your youngest is starting school and your eldest is about to sit the SATS.

If you don't have kids and you don't want to date someone with kids that is fine it's your personal choice but do not write it in your bio. SINGLE MUMS NEED NOT APPLY. Is not a selling point, women without kids will likely see that and think arsehole! If someone with kids messages you then you can simply choose not to reply or say no thank you (On a personal note I'm not judging anyone who won't date someone with kids, like I said it's your choice. But stop for a minute and ask yourself why you won't? A good person is a good person if they're a parent or not. Same as a bad person is a bad person whether or not they're a parent. What is your reasoning? When I was 23 I dated a woman with a five-year-old daughter for a year. It had its challenges. It caused some issues but overall the experience was enriching and far more positive than negative. So ask yourself why? No one is asking you to become a step dad right away, believe me any decent mother will take her time before she considers introducing you to her kids. Why are you limiting your options so much?)

Many years ago A friend of mine showed me the profile of a guy who had messaged her (she did not reply) His opening statement was, "Let me start by stating my love for the beautiful game MAN UTD FAN. Gooners need not apply." Women accept they will become football widows come the FA Cup you don't need to say it. By saying it this guy basically said this is all I have to offer otherwise I'm quite boring, it was a turn off. Saying I like football I support Man Utd is fine if you feel the need to. Note however most women really do not care and it does not need to be said. I like going to football matches would be better. Note the difference between being honest and saying everything!

Avoid negativity. You hate your job, and you want to beat up your boss. You fantasise daily about the dramatic style you'd quit in if you won the lottery. Don't say things like this, instead you have a job but you work to live you don't live to work. Doesn't that sound better?

Try not to brag. I get shown profiles of men who are very up themselves quite often. More often than not it's a turn off or it's attracting the wrong sort of people. If you're wealthy great. Congratulations it's not a bad thing and you have my envy, but don't brag about it. Doing something like that suggests that's all you offer and will only attract gold diggers. Bragging too much about anything else will make you look like a narcissist.

A final thing do not describe yourself as, "a nice guy." The saying nice guys finish last exists for a reason. Think of the person you know who you'd describe as a nice guy everyone knows one. Besides the fact he's really nice why do you describe him as a nice guy? Because it's basically all you have to say about him. Being a nice guy is not a selling point it says you have nothing else to offer. You should be a nice guy be default it is not a feature. You wouldn't apply for a job and say I think

I should have this job because I'm a nice guy would you? No you'd say I should have this job because I have this experience these qualifications and I'm good at it. I've seen it enough times, women are becoming subconsciously conditioned to be turned off on hearing or seeing the words "I'm a nice guy." Nice guys go in the friend-zone.

## The pet peeve box

Now some sites have this or something similar. A part on your profile to describe a pet hate or an unpopular opinion you have. The best advice I can give you in filling something like this out is try to be light-hearted and humorous. This is not the time or place to get political, bash religion, show off, insult someone or portray yourself as a hateful person. Seriously this is the spot where you could undo everything with a single sentence and have someone go from being interested to thinking what an arsehole in seconds. Last time I filled something like this out I wrote something like, "Why don't McDonald's do an all-day breakfast?"

## Your interests

You need to have interests so list some of them. I mean list and I mean some of them. No one wants to see an A4 page worth of bullet points so prioritise.

Say I like fitness and going to the gym. Don't then go on to include your bench press PB, what supplements you take and how you can improve anyone's form.

If you're a gamer say it. Again most women accept that men have a mistress called Xbox or PlayStation. Don't then list your favourite 100 games or what your kill count is on COD.

If you like photography say it. You don't need to go into the specification of your camera, your favourite lenses or how you think Instagram filters suck.

It should flow. Interests: gym and fitness. Gaming, photography etc, etc, etc. A woman should be able to look over it and see you have cool interests, then know you have something in common or something to talk about. They do not need a full breakdown on everything.

## Your perfect match, ideal woman section

Some sites have a section asking you to describe your perfect woman or ideal partner. I know I've just spent a large part of this chapter telling you not to do this but if required there is a right way and a wrong way to do this. Here is what not to do. First off do not make any comparisons. I want a Margot Robbie or Jennifer Lawrence look alike. NO! First off you're coming off very shallow. Secondly the majority of women will think well that is not me and you'll scare them off right away. Imagine if it was the other way around and a woman said I want a Tom Hardy or Ryan Reynolds equivalent? Would that fill you with confidence and make you think yeah I fit the bill?

Do not list physical attributes! Even if you will only date tall blondes with blue eyes and double D's do not say that. Listing these things does not paint you in a good light and the women who match this criteria will probably be turned off because they are sick of hearing it and think that's all you want them for.

Do not use any negative or discriminatory terms. By which I mean, "No feminists," or, "Fatties need not apply," or "I'm not attracted to Asian/black/white women," or "no one over the age of 30." Knowing what you want is important. But statements like this just make you sound like an arsehole, keep it to yourself.

If you have to fill out something like this describe positives. Your ideal woman is "active" or "adventurous" or "a foodie", or she loves the same things you do. You can describe your ideal woman without being a shallow arsehole.

In essence, once you are done your profile should be a few decent photos of you. More than one less than ten. It should contain no more than three to four paragraph's about yourself. You don't want to go into too much detail. You want a woman to read it and become interested in knowing more. If your profile tells all then what is there to talk about in the future? How do you get to know one another if it's all right there? You need to be interesting you need to be appealing. Most important of all you need to leave them wanting more!

Let's go back to an earlier example of this. Say you're a gamer and you've attracted the attention of another gamer. If your profile already states all your favourite games, favourite consoles, high scores etc. Then they know everything. Wouldn't that be much more fun to discuss in person over a drink? The ultimate aim of your profile is to get someone interested enough that they want to go on a date. Not to tell them everything there is to know because then what is the point of having the date?

Final point to make, spell check is your friend! I cannot stress this enough! Spell check then grammar check then upload your profile!

# CHAPTER 4

# Finding someone and sending the first message

So your profile is up and running. Don't expect to sit back and have the women come rolling in. That is not how this works. I touched on this earlier when I said that as a man you will do the vast majority of initial contact. So that means being proactive. I'm assuming you are smart enough to set the search settings on whatever site you've joined to your liking. Now you need to scroll through the results and message those you find appropriate.

As men we are very visual creatures. We will see something we like and we will focus in on it, often ignoring warning signs and red flags. I'm not saying don't pursue anyone you like the look of. After all there is no point in approaching anyone that you have no attraction to. What I'm saying is read the profile that comes with it! Find out if there is more than just a physical appeal. You could potentially be about to message the love of your life. She might be bad news and all kinds of wrong for you, but you don't know because you couldn't be bothered to read a few sentences first. READ THE PROFILE!

Just because someone appeals to you on the visual level it does not mean you are right for each other. All too often as men we are far too willing to look past the obvious flaws because we like what we see and focus in on it.

Let me use buying a car as an example again. You need a car for commuting, shopping, trips away etc. You see a sports car, it looks good you want it. You can barely afford it. The fuel and insurance is going to ruin you. It's impractical, only has two seats and no boot, it's no good for you at all and you know it. But you are willing to ignore all these things because, fuck me it looks so, so, good. Every man has done this or knows someone who has. You need to not fall into that habit and the answer is simple. READ THE PROFILE!

So you've found someone you find attractive, you've read their bio and think you've found common ground. It's time to make contact. Below I'm going to list the do's and don'ts of messaging.

NO DICK PIC! I cannot stress this enough NO DICK PIC'S! No matter how proud you are of what you have they have seen better! They will not be impressed. They are not going to see it and think oh my God it's the penis I've been waiting for my entire life, I must meet this man and have him inside me! You wouldn't walk up to a woman in a bar and just whip it out would you? Why should it be any different on the internet? Come on guys your mother raised you better than that! On the billion to one chance this actually worked ask yourself is this the woman you want to take home and introduce to your family?

DON'T ASK FOR NUDES! Again I cannot stress this enough. It is shocking how many men think this is a perfectly acceptable request in an opening message. If that's what you want there are plenty of websites you can put your credit card into and not waste anyone's time.

Do not just say hi. Or hi how are you? Bear in mind, most attractive women on dating sites will receive in excess of one hundred messages a day. Hi how are you just isn't going to cut it. Fifty other guys already tried that earlier.

No copy and paste messages. Too many men do this. Have a standard message that they copy and paste then send to several women. Changing one or two minor details each time such as the girl's name. Don't do it, it's lazy and it's obvious. They will spot a copied and pasted message a mile off, it's not going to make them feel special or unique, it's not going to make them think you may be a decent guy. Remember women talk and if you're sending an identical message out to multiple women of a similar age in a set area the odds are a few of them know each other. There's a good chance they'll be sitting down one evening with a glass of wine comparing messages they've got (yes women really do this). Then you're busted and you've blown your chances because they will have labelled you an arsehole. Seriously guys it takes a couple of minutes to write a unique individual message to send. If you can't be bothered to do that. Then why should a woman bother to reply to you?

Do not be too forward. Don't message someone for the first time asking to take them out the next day or for their phone number. It can be off putting. Remember this is still the internet the place we were taught to never give our details to strangers or meet up with them. Like it or not right now that's what you are. A stranger on the Internet. You need to build up some rapport first.

Do not copy what it says on your profile. You're making an introduction not sending out your CV. Your message should be enough that she's intrigued and wants to respond, but not so much that she sees it and thinks I can't be bothered to read all of that.

Do not give out your mobile number in your first message. It wreaks of desperation. If you're a high value individual you don't go giving your number to everyone like it's worthless, you give it out only to those you like. Your number should be something she wants to get not have thrown at her.

Do not put yourself down. Again I get shown messages like this all the time. lines like, "I know a guy like me has no chance with a girl as beautiful as you but I just had to try." It does not work! If you don't believe you're good enough for her then why should she think any different? I know you may think you're complimenting her and appearing humble, but you're not. You're making yourself look weak and insecure. Believe me beautiful women receive tonnes of messages like this every day and each time they think, "Yeah you're right." The only women who will like this are the ones who will see you as someone they can use and exploit, don't be that guy.

Do not message someone more than once. Women show me examples of this all the time and believe me they hate it. Once you've messaged someone that's it done. It's now in their hands and there's alone. It is their choice if they want to reply to you, harassing and hounding them about it is never acceptable. Under no circumstances message someone then, a couple of hours later message them again to check if they got your message or ask why they haven't replied. This screams of neediness and desperation, two very unattractive qualities.

Remember attractive women can receive over a hundred messages a day, it is not uncommon for them to take a few days to get round to yours. They might like your message they might reply. But if in the meantime you've messaged them again asking why they haven't replied I guarantee they're not going to.

The military have a term for this with certain missiles. They call it fire and forget. That is how you need to treat any message you send. Once it's sent it is gone forget about it. If you get a response great but if you don't that's the end of it. Do however keep a record of everyone you have messaged. Another thing I get shown all the time from girls is guys messaging them for the first time three or four times. Basically a guy messages so many women he loses track. He forgets that he already messaged them and sends another one. Again they really hate it. It's a huge turn off.

If a woman chooses to ignore your message that is her choice. If she isn't interested or doesn't see an attraction you will not change that! A confident secure man will accept that and move on. Never and I mean NEVER send abusive follow-on messages because you got ignored or rejected. I get shown this all the time, a first message gets followed up by another then another suddenly turning nasty making threats and saying horrible things. Google image search, "rejected men on dating sites." Sadly, there are thousands of examples. This is never acceptable, there is a good chance they will report you and have your account deleted. There is a good chance they'll upload your conversation to the internet for the whole world to see what an arsehole you are. There is a good chance they'll tell everyone they know, remember what I said earlier? Women talk, so do this and half the women you haven't messaged yet already know you for what you are. Ever heard the term digital footprint? It's a trail of bread crumbs you leave on the internet. From your dating profile someone with half a clue can find your Facebook/Linkedin page, from there they can find your parents and siblings Facebook. They can find out who your employer is. They can then share your hateful messages with the ones who raised you and pay you. This has been done before. Many men have ruined themselves because they couldn't handle online rejection. SO DON'T BE AN ARSEHOLE!

If being ignored or rejected is enough to make you

angry and hateful, then clearly you are not in the right frame of mind to be dating. I suggest you take a step back and work through your issues first. Like I said in Chapter 1 the world is a harsh enough place without you adding to it.

"No Negging. For those of you that don't know, negging (derived from the verb neg, meaning 'negative feedback') is an act of emotional manipulation whereby a person makes a deliberate backhanded compliment or otherwise flirtatious remark to another person to undermine their confidence and increase their need of the manipulator's approval." – Wikipedia

Negging is a form of manipulation. That's all you really need to know. I've had plenty of friends tell me that it works, but you haven't even met this woman yet do you really want to start off by playing mind games? Plus this isn't something new, women are wising up to this and when they realise what you're doing and catch you out they will not be impressed.

So what should you say? The truth is I don't know, there is no magic code. If you haven't figured it out yet every woman is unique, what's right for one isn't for another. You need to figure this out and customise what you are going to say accordingly after all you're the one who has seen her profile and read her bio.

Say hello, ask a question or two about an interest she has, or an interest you share that show's you've actually read her profile. Pay her a compliment if you like, but don't come on too strong, again it can make you appear needy. If complimenting I'd try to avoid complimenting them. Say there is a picture of them on holiday. I wouldn't compliment them saying. "you looked very beautiful on that boat." I'd compliment the actual the trip itself and say, "the scenery from that boat is beautiful, looks like an amazing place." If she's beautiful she knows she is. You as a stranger telling her so is unoriginal and comes across as little more than a worthless comment to seek her approval. Keep it short and simple one or two paragraph's at most. Any more than that you're coming on too strong and trying too hard. Avoid all negativity. If you've noted a mutual interest make it interesting. If they like running don't just say, "I like running too." Ask them if they've entered any races this year have they ever thought about doing a tough mudder? Don't just say look at my profile I think we have a lot in common. (that's not trying hard enough) If they are interested they will look trust me. The key is to pique their interest and leave them wanting more. At the end sign off with your name. This way they see you as a person not just another username on a screen.

Alternatively you may see something on a profile that instantly catches your eye and you can just send a quick message to start a conversation about it. Now the more interesting it is the better this will work. Let's say a girl is wearing a *Star Wars* T- shirt in a photo and it's caught your eye. Sending her a quick message saying, "I love *Star Wars*." Doesn't give her much to work with or reply to. Be more original, "Jedi or Sith?" Think outside the box, make her want to reply. The best example I can give of a quick message working I heard third hand, so I cannot guarantee it's 100% true but it sounded good so here it is.

A girl had a selfie of her at a Foo Fighters concert at Milton Keynes bowl and a guy sent her a message saying, "Hey though it's a little fuzzy I'm the guy in the far right-hand corner of your photo in the blue shirt." Of course chances like that coming up are slim to none but you get the idea.

Now that you've sent your first message what should you do next? Message someone else. Internet dating is a numbers game. You will not get a response from every message you send. From the responses you do get conversations will fizzle out and dry up long before you meet in person. The more women you message the greater your chances. I need to be clear on this I'm still championing quality over quantity. Find profiles you like, read them and write them a message. I'm not suggesting you message every woman in a twenty-mile radius.

And of course do not forget, keep a record of everyone you've messaged. Never forget spell check is your friend!

## Liking profiles/poking/nudging/winking/waving and other features

With the exception of apps like tinder where the whole point is to swipe to like or dislike profiles. I suggest avoiding features like this on dating sites Many sites offer something similar where you can click through profile pictures, liking or disliking. The owner of said picture then gets a notification if you liked their photo. Features like this were originally designed for the benefit of women. They see a profile they like and can send a signal which says to the guy I'm not opposed to receiving a message from you. If you receive one of these notifications and like who sent it to you then great carry on. But I wouldn't suggest sending out these notifications yourself. While it's the 21st century and we are all equal, gender roles are still very much alive. You as the man are expected to do the work. Do not expect results just from clicking like on someone's profile. It suggests you lack the confidence to actually talk to them or make the first move. (an unattractive quality) Also it's lazy and laziness just won't do. There will be no shortage of men messaging her, what makes you think you'll come out on top if the best you can do is like a picture?

Once you've sent your messages then what? Log off and get on with your day. Go out, live your life. Don't sit there looking at your inbox refreshing the page, you'll drive yourself insane. Some sites offer features to allow you to see when your message has been read or deleted. Avoid this like the plague. This is the behaviour of a needy man who requires validation. That's not who you want to be. Remember what I said fire and forget.

# CHAPTER 5

# You've got mail

So you've received a message, maybe you've received several. So far so good but it's still early doors, don't get too ahead of yourself. I say this because I remember exactly how I was the first time I got a message. Being as awkward as I was and believing I had no value to women it was a moment of disbelief. I couldn't believe there was a woman who was interested in me. I focused in on her, got ahead of myself and jumped the gun completely. Now for the love of God don't be like I was. Read this chapter carefully. This has been learnt from experience!

First I need to state this before we go into anything else because you cannot forget it. The point of this is to get a date! I'm going to repeat that sentence a lot in this chapter because the goal of this is to get a date, not a pen pal. You can't allow yourself to forget that. The most important thing I need to tell you though is to enjoy yourself! If you're anything like I was women actually wanting to talk to me was shocking. So enjoy it, you can be desired you can have a good time and you should.

## How soon should you respond to the message?

Movies have always taught us that the cool guys wait three days before calling a girl. Maybe it's true and it works I don't know, but this is real life not a movie. The world has changed, this is the digital age. We all have smart phone's, were all connected to the internet by them, we get instant notifications and our phones are always in our hands. In these movies the girl has given her number to the guy in person so they can make a date. In doing so she has already shown him a high level of attraction and he has been able to read that. You do not have this luxury online.

I advise you not to reply immediately though. Appearing too keen and eager is not a good thing. You're an interesting guy right? You've got a job, you've got friends you've listed your hobbies and interests on your profile. If she gets a reply from you within 30 seconds it's not exactly selling that image of you very well is it. Also it is important not to rush. You should take the time to get it right. Read the message properly, decide if you want to reply then write an appropriate reply. Remembering spell check is your friend.

The only rule I set on replying to a message was, I would never stop what I was doing to reply. The message could wait until I was finished. For example if I was at work even if I had nothing to do I would wait for my break before replying. If the message was sent 3 hours or 20 minutes before my break it didn't matter. If I was out with some friends, even once I had a decent phone and every dating site had an app instead of me having to log onto a computer if I got a message, it could wait until I got home or back to my car. Imagine a CEO in a meeting. He wouldn't stop the meeting on his multi-million deal to message a girl would he? No, he's a high value individual and wouldn't put his world on hold. Well remember CEO or not you are a high value individual too because you have self-worth. Dropping everything to reply instantly does not give off that impression.

Think of it another way imagine a girl has several guys messaging her. They are all very keen and replying instantly. But you don't, you're not ignoring her but you're taking your time because you have a life. That makes you stand out. She's going to see all these other men messaging her and wonder why aren't you, what makes you different? You've clearly got something else going on outside of a dating site. That will raise her level of interest. These other guys clearly have nothing else to do that makes them easy and boring. By default you are the most interesting of the group.

This is a lesson I learnt the hard way. As I said earlier when I started I had little to no self-worth when it came to dealing with women. At first if a woman messaged me I would drop everything because HOLY SHIT a WOMAN messaged me. I would reply instantly then wonder why after a couple of messages it quickly went dead. Dropping everything to reply to a stranger and appear at their beck and call is the behaviour of a weak and needy man. Women do not respect weak or needy men!

## Building a rapport

It is essential that you take time to build up a rapport before doing anything like trying to get her phone number or asking her out on a date. Don't ask me how long because there isn't a set time! Building a rapport depends on the two of you and takes as long as it takes. No woman will want to meet anyone until they feel comfortable, coming on too strong or pressuring them will not achieve this. Remember though the aim is to get a date not a pen pal, leave it too long the conversation will die off and no date. How quickly you build a rapport depends on the frequency that you message each other, it depends on how well your conversation is going. I've asked women out after two weeks I've asked women out after one day because the conversation was going well and I was able to work into it nicely. There is no point asking until you are confident they are going to say yes. If someone is interested but you've asked too soon there is a good chance they won't say yes the second time either because the first time likely put them off.

I cannot tell you how to judge this and know when the time is right. It's you in the conversation you need to figure it out yourself and gauge their interest correctly. This can be tricky online, you can't read body language I can offer you a few tips though. When messaging try not to talk about yourself. Ask them questions instead. If she wants to know about you she will ask. If she's asking questions about you then she's interested. If she's openly telling you things and answering your questions she's probably interested. Blunt to the point answers probably not so much.

Pick up on the hints. For example If you tell her you went to the new restaurant/cocktail bar that just opened up and she responds saying, "I just heard about that place I'd really like to go." That suggests she's not against you taking her there. If she wasn't she'd be texting her girlfriends and saying hey there's a new cocktail place open lets go, not saying it to you.

I learnt to seize these moments, but for a long time I was oblivious to them. The amount of subliminal messages I missed is horrifying, the list of women who ghosted me because I didn't take the hint is long. Fortunately I was adaptable to change. If a woman mentioned a place she liked or wanted to try I would use that as my opening provided I felt there was enough of a rapport. "Great, when are you free for me to take you for food/drinks there?" This proved to be my preferred and most successful method. It works nicely into the conversation, it's not too in your face. It's open so if you've made the mistake and asked too soon all is not necessarily lost. It's not aggressive but it's not weak either. The intentions of the message are very clear. "I want to take you out on a date."

Note my exact words here. I never asked a woman out "for a date." It sounds so serious and formal doesn't it. It's meant to be exciting and fun. I never asked "if" of "maybe" Another thing women get all the time and don't like are date invites that go like this. "Well IF you are free, MAYBE you would like to go out some time IF you want to?" If you don't sound convinced why should she be? Notice the difference? A woman is still welcome to say no the way I did it but at least I'm not suggesting she says no myself. I didn't ask are you free Friday? You don't know much about her life at this point, you definitely don't know her schedule, there's a good chance she's not free Friday or whatever day you asked, then it gets awkward and you have to ask her out again. Don't ask me why it gets awkward it just does even if you're both into each other.

Of course there are hundreds of ways you can ask her out. that's just what I found worked best for me. Just remember you need to build a rapport you need to gauge their level of interest and you need to ask when the timing is right. When you both know enough about each other that you're no longer strangers. You're comfortable enough to meet but both still want to know more.

## Getting Ghosted

*Ghosting is a colloquial term used to describe the practice of ceasing all communication and contact with a partner, friend, or similar individual without any apparent warning or justification and subsequently ignoring any attempts to reach out or communication made by said partner, friend, or individual. The term originated in the early 2000s. In the following decade, media reported a rise in ghosting, which has been attributed to the increasing use of social media and online dating apps.* – Wikipedia

Being ghosted isn't a good feeling but in the world of online dating it will happen to you sooner or later. Most of the time you'll have no idea why. Things could seem very promising then suddenly nothing. I wouldn't bother trying to contact them again asking why, they're already ignoring you as it is. Besides that is not the actions of a strong, confident man, you can't let it bother you. There are hundreds of possible explanations none of which really concern you. Just move on.

## Giving out or asking for phone numbers

Usually an exchange of numbers is likely to happen before a first date. After all most people prefer to take things away from the dating site sooner rather than later. As I've already said don't just throw it at them as soon as you can. Something given away that freely has no value. She should want to get your number not have it thrust upon her. In turn she should want you to have her number not have you demand it.

Let me give you a real example of a time I went wrong in my days of low self-worth. A woman had messaged me. Not replied to me, but found my profile and messaged me herself. I remember she was very pretty, had lovely long hair and some of the longest legs I had ever seen. Most importantly she loved wild camping. Literally my favourite thing. Of course I went off the deep end focused in on her and became the guy I've been telling you not to be. We were messaging for a couple of days one or two messages a day at most. They were good messages though and so far everything seemed promising. At the end of the week I was going wild camping for four nights. So I told her I was going away wild camping and said, "I won't have any internet so here's my number, text me." I never got any texts but two days later we returned to civilisation for more supplies and I check my profile. I had a message from her ignoring that I've given her my number and just replying to the rest of the message I'd sent two days ago. So I message her again saying, "Hey just back in the real world for a few minutes I only just got this message as no internet where I'm camped, here's my number again text me." I never did get a text from her, when the trip was over I never received another message from her on the dating site either.

Now there are hundred's or possible reasons why I was ghosted. But these are the simple facts we know. We had only been speaking for a couple of days, exchanged less than ten messages when I tried to give her my number without her wanting it. Now didn't that make me look desperate. Didn't that make having my number worthless, throwing it at strangers like that. No wonder she didn't want it. Didn't I come across needy, desperately trying to stay in contact with her even though I was going away on a holiday! No wonder she didn't text me She probably didn't want someone who came across as needy as I did back then having her number. Block number wasn't a standard feature on most phones at the time. Giving her my number so soon was a mistake. Not a deal breaker but still a mistake. Messaging her from the middle of my trip and giving it to her again though was probably the nail in the coffin.

What I should have done was say to her I'm going wild camping for a week I'll message you when I'm back off the moors, then gone offline. She would have known I was away doing something she found very interesting, I wouldn't have come across as weak or needy and she probably would have been excited to hear from me again the next week because she would have been interested to know what I had been up to. At which point I could have said, "Yeah it was a very good trip, when are you free to meet up for a drink? I'd love to tell you all about it." That would have led to a natural exchange of numbers.

Giving her your number or asking for hers? There is a lot of debate as to which one is better with so called experts, psychologists and pick up artists on either side of the fence. Personally, I prefer to ask for hers, once I feel the conversation has progressed enough for me to ask for it. I prefer this because it's a good indicator of her interest. It goes back to what I said about confidence and self-worth again. What makes you appear stronger? Having the balls to ask for hers or just giving yours and hoping? The perfect scenario of course is you both exchange numbers because you have set up a date.

Once you have her number do not contact her through the dating site again. It will lead to only one thought in her head. "I gave him my number why is he on here?" It works both ways if you see her online on the site as well. The fact is neither of you are doing anything wrong by still talking to other people, neither of you owe one another anything. But it can be a sore point so don't do it. Definitely don't message her on the dating site once you've been calling or texting asking her what she's doing because you saw she was online. That makes you look very insecure.

## What not to do with a woman's number

Do not call her to check the number is real. Some men really do this, it screams insecurity, it's a huge turn off. Unless the last message you got said something along the lines of, "Yes I'd love to, here's my number call me now and we will arrange a date for tomorrow," don't call her right away. If you haven't exchanged numbers but have hers then send her a text with your name so she has your number as well. If you've already set up a date leave it at that. If you haven't then hopefully if she's interested enough she will save your number and answer when you call to set up a date.

Do not go near her number if you've been drinking. She doesn't know you yet, a slurred voicemail at one in the morning is not endearing. A badly spelt text about how you hope she likes you because you want to smash her back doors in won't score you any points either.

Don't get caught in endless text conversation. This is more of a problem for the younger generations but I see it all the time, bad first dates that don't lead to a second one, followed by a dumb comment like, "I don't get it we were texting all the time I thought we would hit it off." The point was to get a date not a pen pal. If you engage in constant texting what will you have to talk about in person? Wouldn't you much rather get to know someone and grow attraction face to face than through a screen? The same principles I mentioned earlier in this chapter apply here.

Don't get caught up in long phone calls. Same problems and principles as above. You want to talk to her in person not over the phone, if she wants to be on the phone for hours she has her best friends for that. Don't fall into that category. Keep phone calls short and sweet don't let them drag on until you both have nothing to say, it will lead to boring and unsuccessful dates. Remember you are a high value interesting guy with a life. Being available for two-hour long phone calls or being free to text all day suggests the opposite.

By no means ignore them. Don't be rude, but the objective of texting or calling for you is to set dates, not enter the friend zone.

## Social media and friend requests

As well as exchanging numbers you may get asked for your Facebook, Twitter, Instagram etc. Like I said this is the digital age, it's the preferred form of communication for some. Most likely scenario though if they're asking for your social media they are being nosy and want a good stalk before meeting you. They want to see if they know anyone you know, they want to see your less flattering pictures, they want to see if there are any photos of your ex, they want to know any ugly little detail you may not have offered. Some women will be very open and honest about this and ask to add you or just add you. (It works both ways of course you can accept a friend request depending how curious you are to see what's on their profiles?) Some will be more covert about it. I had a woman once ask my last name. Two minutes later she asked me how I knew Zoe? (Turns out we had a mutual friend.) Personally, I do not like it. If anyone asks I tell them I don't add anyone I haven't met. Mainly because I don't need my mother, aunts and cousins asking, "Ooooooh, who is she?" But other than that I refuse because like I said a bit of mystery is good. If you're part of the social media generation and you're comfortable to gain a new friend/follower go for it, but don't add them if you don't want to.

When we start talking to someone from a dating site and learn their full name I'm sure we are all guilty of looking up their social media profiles and seeing what we can. My advice to you though is not to send them an unprompted friend request or start following them without warning. Even though she has undoubtedly stalked you online, a surprise friend request will make her think you're a crazy stalker. My advice over all keep away from social media with each other until you've met in person and know you like one another.

## Talking to more than one woman

I've said it already, internet dating is a numbers game, and you don't owe anyone anything at this point. For me this was an incredibly new experience and at first it made me feel guilty. If that happens to you get over it. You're doing nothing wrong and you're very naive if you think any woman you're talking to isn't talking to other men as well. (She is also doing nothing wrong.) If and when it happens enjoy it, it's an excellent confidence boost. However be careful. This is an area where it is very easy to mess up. Make sure you keep track of who is who, don't mix people up and say something meant for someone else. Saying the wrong thing to the wrong person is an easy mistake to make and one there is no coming back from.

## Making the right choice for you

This is for those of you who are like I used to be. When I first started online dating in my time of low self-worth I responded to everyone and met women I shouldn't have. I went on dates with women who I had no attraction to or interest in. Essentially wasting my time and theirs. This isn't a dig at those women, I'm sure there is someone out there for each of them but it definitely wasn't me. Because of my low self-esteem I couldn't seem to say no. This is because I was not thinking about myself, any woman who showed an interest in me must be OK. I never stopped to think about what I wanted or what was good for me. This is also important, just because someone is messaging you it doesn't mean you have to reply or engage in conversation if it's not for you. I even ended up in some very short-lived relationships because my self-esteem was low enough to make me believe I'd do no better than any woman who talked to me. This whole process is as much about you as it is them, remember what I said in Chapter two and don't settle. Just because they've talked to you it doesn't mean you have to date them.

## Red flags and warning signs

When I was much younger, awkward and lacking self-esteem, if a girl was messaging me that was all I needed to know. This meant although I noticed them I chose to ignore several red flags and alarms that said I wasn't talking to a good person or at least not someone who was a good match for me. If something sets off alarm bells for you I'm not suggesting you drop everything and cease contact. However don't ignore it, keep your eyes open so it doesn't blindside you later on. Here are some of the more common ones to watch out for.

## The photos are just too good

The photos all appear professionally done, this means you might not be talking to the person in the pictures. This isn't always the case, a lot of women get photo-shoots done but be cautious. if you are suspicious Google, "How to do a reverse image search." If those photos have been taken from the internet you'll soon know. Most scammers use photos of catalogue models or porn stars (with their clothes still on) stolen from other sites.

It may just be you're talking to a beautiful woman

with professionally taken photos. Be wary though if she starts asking you questions like your postcode, date of birth and mother's maiden name. You've got a scammer.

You may also receive a message from a profile with photo's like this from a girl who actively admits she does porn. The message is copied pasted and sent to everyone in a 50-mile radius. It's advertising, nothing more, she is looking for more customers and website traffic to pay subscription fees. If you want to pay the charge to see her play with herself on cam that's your choice. But don't waste your time messaging and trying to talk to her, she is not remotely interested.

## No photos at all

Personally, I wouldn't respond to a message from an account with no photos even if the message lit up every nerve ending in my brain. If a profile has no photos then it's one of these things. Not a genuine account. The account of someone already in a relationship that doesn't want to get caught by their partner or partner's friends. Someone with such low self-esteem they couldn't put a picture up. Someone who isn't even remotely serious, so a complete waste of time.

## The high angled or cropped photo

This is a tactic employed by overweight women and those with body confidence issues. You may come across profiles where the photos are all selfies taken with the camera held as high as possible over the woman's head. They do this because it offers a more flattering angle and helps hide the fact they're overweight. Now everyone will stack the deck in their favour when it comes to picking the photos they put on their profile, it's a given. There is nothing wrong with that, none of us are going to choose unflattering photos are we? Let me be perfectly clear I am not fat shaming. I'm not saying you shouldn't date anyone bigger than a size 12. The problem here is not that a woman may be large or overweight, the problem is they may not be honest about it, they may be very deceitful about it and when you meet you'll find they have misrepresented themselves. This has happened to me before, the fact the woman in question was overweight wasn't the problem. The problem was I had been deceived, it made me wonder, how could I trust this woman if she was lying to me from the very beginning? This works both ways of course. Most women like tall men, now if you're below the average height you might claim an extra inch on your profile, but don't say you're over 6ft if you're really 5'8" because you cannot hide the truth when you meet in person.

Now I appreciate that someone with body confidence issues is very likely struggling with their self-esteem. Hence why they may be less than honest with their description. But I've said already I want a woman with confidence. A self-esteem issue that's serious enough to make you lie as well was a red flag for me. I have dated plenty of plus sized women in the past. The difference was they accepted who they were and they owned it.

## Beware of the wannabe influencer

This sort of profile is similar to the profile of the woman who actively admits to being a cam girl or sex worker, but they don't admit to anything. You might get a message from or find the profile of a beautiful girl. It will probably be a well written profile, but the profile will lead to an Instagram account or similar link. If you message them you'll probably get a nice message back but it finishes with a line like, "I'm not on here very much, follow me on Instagram, message me on that I check that more." Don't waste your time! This woman is not interested in dating she just wants more followers and more likes. She has figured out that dating sites and apps are full of men only too happy to follow her social media accounts and like every selfie she uploads. Follow her if you want, don't bother trying to message her though she's leading you as well as hundreds of other men on.

## The one that admits to being a horrible bitch

You'll come across profiles like this, usually she's very attractive and she knows it. Her bio will literally be a list of reasons not to date her, it will read something like; "I'm spoilt, impatient, crazy, better than you, I demand to be treated like a princess, I won't message you back unless (Insert list of unrealistic demands.) You couldn't handle me anyway." This isn't comedy, she isn't being sarcastic or ironic. But for some reason men love bitches (It's a best-selling book look it up). Well that's not entirely true. Men love strong women, we just have difficulty telling the difference. This is not the profile of a strong woman it's the profile of a horrible one. This profile should be avoided because she was telling the truth, yet so many men are drawn to it like some sort of challenge. Pursue it if you must but don't say I didn't warn you.

## Beware of gold-diggers

Be aware some women are only interested in exploiting you. Of course they all want a wealthy man for this but they usually have no qualms about rinsing a working-class guy either. Look out for warning signs like their level of interest changing when certain things like money come up. I know someone who told me every woman's interest level jumps when he tells them he's the director of a company. That's only natural a successful motivated guy is attractive. But he is always very wary of the ones who hardly give him the time of day until they find out what he does. Asking what you do for a living is a normal question. Asking how much you make is not.

I've been ghosted by some women after they have asked my occupation and realised I'm not in a highly paid industry. On the other side I've noticed women suddenly becoming overly keen when they hear I own my house and do not rent it. Pick up on other tells they have. Do you have a gold Rolex on in your picture, did they notice that before anything else? Or did they notice that holiday photo is a very exclusive resort? Sometimes there is no fool proof way of knowing until you meet them, and I like to give people the benefit of the doubt. But don't let yourself be exploited.

## Watch out for the unstable

In chapter four I said there are men who need to work through their issues before online dating, that's something that goes both ways. There are a lot of women online who really have no business dating until they sort through their shit. You need to be aware of the warning signs. Look out for any heavy negativity. You're looking for someone to enjoy life with, not drag you down. If they're unhappy with their friends, unhappy with their job, unhappy with their home, unhappy with their life. Clearly they are not in the right frame of mind for this. But they believe meeting someone and no longer being single will solve all their problems. It won't! You will not be their knight in shining armour, so get the romantic notion of riding in to save her out of your head it doesn't work. Sure maybe going out on dates and having fun will make her feel happier, but it doesn't take away the core issues that are waiting for her to go home to as soon as the date is over. If this is what they are like online, what do you think they'll be like in person? Usually dating someone like this is not fun. Because misery loves company, she will most likely drag you down or resent you for being happy. That's not always the case of course but if you choose to date someone like this go in with your eyes open and know when to walk away if needs be.

I remember once a girl messaged me, over all she seemed quite nice. But in her second message she told me she didn't allow either of her ex's to see their kids as they were both worthless nasty bastards. This told me she was very bitter about it, in a very broken home life and had some serious issues that I wanted no part of. Especially if she was so desperate to offer up this information unprompted in her second message. I wished her luck with that and moved on. Even if she had been perfect in every other way I wanted no part of it. At the very least it sounded like there was a psycho ex liable to show up at any moment and want to smash your head in. Now sure she deserves to find love as much as anyone else, and I hope she has but she wasn't going to find anything with anyone until her issues were sorted.

## Watch out for rebounders and those not over their ex

Women rebound very differently to men. When I broke up with my last ex despite her crying and begging me not to, promising me she would change, pledging her undying love to me and swearing she would never cheat or be horrible ever again she was back on the market within 24-hours. She had hooked up and slept with someone within 72-hours. I know all this because she told me on the phone as she was driving away from the guy's place, like it was a competition or she wanted to try and hurt me. That's what she did to get over it, I logged out of all my social media and went scuba diving for three weeks. We do things very differently.

Women on the rebound come with excess baggage and some are only good for sex. I know some of you may now be thinking great I'll only go for women on the rebound. It isn't good sex though, there will be no connection and it won't be you she's thinking of. Many women rebounding gravitate to the polar opposite of their ex, meaning you're probably not her type. Which means anything you have will probably be short lived because you two are not a good fit for one another. Again you will not be her knight in shining armour and save her from herself, she is there for herself and herself alone. She will probably make a string of bad decisions until she gets it out of her system. If you want to be one of those bad decisions that's on you, but don't get caught up and hurt because of it, know what you're getting into.

How will you know if a woman's rebounding? She will likely tell you. Not in those exact words of course but she will make it obvious enough. Her ex will keep coming up in conversation, you'll likely receive very mixed signals from the messages she sends. One minute she may be overly keen, the next she may seem cold and distant. This is because her emotions are all over the place. She will say things like, "I'm not looking for anything serious", then talk long term plans and commitments. This is because she is mixing up her emotions and feelings she still has for her ex with the current situation she finds herself in, or she is creating a fantasy world planning a future she will never have with you, the guy she just met to distract her from where she finds herself. These fantasy worlds don't last long, they soon come tumbling down.

A woman who isn't over her ex is a potential flight risk. The odds are they are still in contact and she wants him back. There seems to be no such thing as a clean break these days. This is someone likely to suddenly ghost you. If you do meet and date them don't be surprised if you suddenly get dropped with no warning because she has gone back to him.

# CHAPTER 6

# Making a date

You've asked her out, she's said yes and you've exchanged numbers great. What's next? The first thing I'd do is back off. Unless she contacts me I will now typically minimise contact. If it's Tuesday and we've agreed to meet Friday I will say, "Great I'm looking forward to meeting you Friday, see you then." I will then keep contact via phone calls or texts to a minimum. Like I said I want something to talk about, you're making it more difficult for yourself if you've both had a play by play of each other's week building up to Friday. I know to some this may sound counter-productive when it was going so well. I'm not telling you to ghost them. I'm telling you to back off if they contact you by all means reply. But trust me this helps to build and maintain interest in you. Have a bit of mystery, create some anticipation, let her wonder what you're doing you want her to be excited to meet you after all. Resist the temptation to contact her to check the date is still on. It's insecure, a confident guy won't worry about that. You want to project the image of someone so confident you have no fear of being stood up. If she contacts you to check the date is still on say, "Of course I'm a man of my word."

I once dated a woman From Poland and she was stunning. So much so that when we first made contact I thought I was being catfished. We arranged to meet after work one night then I backed off completely. Not because I knew what I was doing at the time but because I didn't think it was real. Two days later she messaged me asking if I had lost interest and was worrying I wasn't going to show up. My behaviour had increased her interest and attraction to me. Removing my attention had increased hers. Looking the way she did she was used to guys hounding her. We met she wasn't a catfish and we had a lot of fun during our time together.

## Where to go what to do?

Most dating experts and pick up artists will tell you to now take control. You decide where you are going, most suggest not even telling her. it's a surprise you arrange to pick her up and take her out. Movies have told us you need to do something to blow her mind take her somewhere no other guy has ever thought of, I'm going to suggest the exact opposite. First of all it's very unlikely you'll be picking her up at her front door this is real life not a teen rom-com. You're still a stranger from the internet So when she asks where are we going and you say it's a surprise you sound like a potential serial killer. Doing something amazing and blowing her mind on the first date also translates to trying too hard. If you're a multimillionaire and you usually have lunch in the most exclusive restaurant in the city cool, go for it. If you've never been there before and you're about to blow your entire month's pay on one date to try and impress her, you are not offering her the real you and she will see straight through that.

My aim on a first date is to make a woman feel safe and comfortable. So usually I'll offer to meet a woman somewhere they can feel safe and comfortable. I'll ask them, "where is somewhere that's familiar for you where you'll be cool with meeting me?" If further explanation is needed I'll tell them, "as a man I'm not concerned for my safety but I appreciate that it's different for women." So I don't mind travelling and meeting them in a setting they are happy with. This is an area most men disagree with me they tell me things like I'm giving up my masculine power by doing this or I'm being a beta male or a feminist. (Call me a feminist all you want by the way I won't be insulted by that) Try to see this from a woman's point of view, if you can't see my point Google search, "What would you do if there were no men on earth for 24-hours." Read the results it is not pretty. This is the world we have created gentlemen, don't be an arsehole and add to it!

The reason so many people disagree with me on this is because if you're not careful you appear indecisive. Indecisive is not good. It's a trait of everything you're trying not to be. I'm sure we've all been there before with a previous girlfriend. (What do you want to do? I don't mind what do you want to do? I don't mind either, OK well you choose?) We've all had conversations like that. They're not good. As a man you need to be decisive and make decisions, even if it's a bad decision it's better than saying, "Oh I don't mind," because that does not project strength and confidence she wants you to make the decision. There is a smart way of doing this of course Google is your friend again. You're talking to this woman you know what her home town is so type it into the search bar look what's there. Look what's in the surrounding towns and villages. Read some reviews. When you offer to meet her at a location that's comfortable for her and she then suggests her home town or a nearby place you can say oh I know a nice place there called whatever, let's meet there. That way safe and comfortable for her and you weren't indecisive.

Once you've decided on a location, you need to decide on a place. my preferred place for a first date was always a coffee shop. There's a drink in there for everyone, there are always other people (witnesses) and they are usually located on high streets or in town centres (populated area's) So if either of you think, fuck me this person is a lunatic, a safe get away can be made. I usually try to avoid pubs as a first meeting place, it can make your brain over think. Should I drink, should I not? What if she doesn't drink? What is she going to think if I drink at this time of day? Then there's the chance of some drunken idiot coming onto your date. (yes this really has happened to me before. I'll explain how to deal with something like that later in the book) Also the best pubs for date settings, the one's with comfy chairs and big log fires are usually located in the countryside on isolated roads. Not ideal for making her feel comfortable meeting a stranger or your safe getaway if needed.

I know a coffee shop may sound boring but consider this first part more of an interview, you are both seeing if you like each other's company enough to want to enjoy doing something else together. The coffee shop is the ideal setting to figure that out. It doesn't have to end there if you are both having a good time.

One of the best first dates I ever had started in a coffee shop, we hit it off. She mentioned she wasn't a huge fan of this chain coffee shop and much preferred the smaller independent one further in town. So I got up and said, "Grab your coat, what are we doing here?" We made our way through town to the next coffee shop where we continued to hit it off. Then I asked if the Italian we had passed was any good? We should share a pizza. From the Italian she took me to a pub she liked, there we had a couple of drinks got comfy and kissed each other. This happened because she was feeling safe and comfortable with me. By moving on from the coffee shop and doing our mini tour of her home town I essentially took her on four dates in one. This made it more fun, kept her interest and attraction levels up and I made very good progress.

Of course coffee shop isn't a rule, it was just my preference, find what works for you and find what works for your date. My only advice is you want a setting or experience where you get to know each other first time. By all means plan something more exciting but you want to be able to talk and get to know each other. Things like cinema's and concerts can be counter-productive to this.

## She said no or made an excuse

It happens. Not everyone will say yes. Don't take it personally. Remember what I said a confident and secure man will move on and not be offended. You'll get told things like, "I would but I'm just so busy at the moment. Or my mum's in town or I'm unwell or I don't know if you and I will be a good match." The list goes on. It is important to not let this get you down, it happens. When it happens simply say, "OK, well you have my number if anything changes give me a call." Then leave it do not contact them again. If they've blown you off with a line like, "I would but I'm just too busy," don't then ask well what about next week instead or start offering other days that you're free, you're coming across desperate. Same again just say, "OK, well why don't you give me a call when you're not too busy," then don't contact them again. Sometimes they genuinely are busy, other times they can be testing you. If they are testing you the strong response is the one where you don't become desperate and remain unfazed by it.

There can be many reasons a woman says no, not all of them are because of you. You don't know what her mindset is. Maybe she has very low self-esteem and is too nervous. Maybe she's only online dating to make an ex jealous and get him back.

Maybe she doesn't know what she wants and is just looking. Maybe she's just attention seeking. A friend of mine has tinder on her phone but in all the time I've known her she has never met a guy once. When I asked her what the deal was she told me she just likes having a busy phone. This is why you can't take it personally or let it get you down. This is also why I told you online dating is a numbers game.

## She cancelled last minute

Again it happens sometimes. Another reason why I suggest a coffee shop. It's far less annoying having that date cancelled than if you've gone out and bought tickets to something. Sometimes there are legitimate reasons, sometimes you're getting messed around. Same principles apply don't get mad at them but do not allow yourself to be messed around either. "Let me know when you're free and we can reschedule." Then don't contact them again. Some women will push you to see what they can get away with and how you'll respond. Again the strong response is not to go chasing after them. Personally if I thought a woman was doing this on a first date I wouldn't bother trying for a second. You'll know a decent woman because if she has to cancel she will make the effort to reschedule. She won't if you get mad and become an arsehole about it though.

## Being stood up

Being stood up sucks. I'll tell you not to take it personally but you will if it happens. It's hard not to. Sometimes there is a legitimate reason and later on you'll receive a very apologetic message. Though legitimate reasons are few and far between now we all have smart phones. As unlikely as they are, car crashes, family members suddenly having heart attacks, etc., can happen. If I got stood up I would not waste my time trying to reschedule I wouldn't contact them. But if you do get that apologetic message or call and you think it sounds legit it's down to you. Do not stand for it a second time though.

## She wants to bring a friend or invites you out with her friendship group

You might get asked something like this, simply put the answer is no. She asks if she can bring a friend? Don't get excited this isn't the prelude to a threesome. There can be many reasons for this but usually it's because she's not sure if she's going to like you so she asks if a friend can come so she has a way out. Or as you're a stranger on the internet it's a security thing. Don't agree to it. First of all even if you two really hit it off, you will be hindered by the third person there it will be awkward as hell. If you two are kind of hitting it off but it could go either way having the third person there will make it go the wrong way. No good will ever come from this situation That third person isn't looking to date you so they will naturally be looking to find things not to like about you. So even if you and your date are a match made in heaven after your date the friend will likely be saying did you notice this did you notice that? Of course don't say, "No they can't come." Instead say something like, "Look I thought we were going out me and you, if that's a problem because you're with your friend let me know another time you're free and we can reschedule." Agreeing to something like this makes you look weak again because you are being a pushover before you have even met her. It's failing another test.

You might get something like, well me and a few of my friends will be at such and such a place at this time why don't you come down and meet me there? Again simply put the answer is no. Do not accept invitations like this, again there can be several reasons for an invite like this, it may be a security thing, she may have a very busy social life and think she's killing two birds with one stone. It may be she's not sure how into you she is and thinks this encounter will be less awkward than a date if she's not sure. You haven't met her yet why would you want to meet her friends? Situations like this can be nothing other than awkward and uncomfortable. What I said in the previous paragraph about looking for reasons not to like you, well now you have a whole crowd doing it, not just one person. If it's a mixed group of friends odds are there is at least one guy present who's been friend zoned. So essentially you've accepted an invite that comes with its own cock block. A date is for you two to meet and get to know each other, end of story. Same as before, decline and offer to reschedule. Let me reiterate If she's suggesting things like this because she's unsure. It likely means her interest or attraction level isn't that high for her to want to date you. Agreeing it to this won't raise her interest levels. The same goes for double dates. Double dates should only occur once you're an established couple. Just no!

## What should I wear?

Well you've been dressing yourself for your entire

adult life, you should be able to figure this out easily enough. Yes you should make an effort but you still need to be yourself. Don't put on the suit you last wore to a wedding for a date, if next week you'll go on a second date in jeans, trainers and a T-shirt. You no doubt have your own style and what you like, stick with it be an honest representation of you. Pick from the nicer end or your wardrobe rather than the casual end sure but don't go mad. Make sure your clothes are clean. Dirty clothes are a no, this also goes for footwear. If you are meeting after work, or something else, go home and change first. A friend of mine once got turned down for a second date because while she liked him she was unimpressed he showed up in his couriers uniform. The same goes for showing up in something like your Sunday league football kit after a game. Go home SHOWER and change first. Avoid T-shirts with writing on. Yes I'm sure it's hilarious and got laughs down the pub but you may come across immature. Track suits and sweat pants can also suggest the same, as well as a complete lack of effort. What I would do is imagine there was a club bouncer I had to get past to get to my date. If I wasn't dressed appropriately then he wouldn't let me in. The most important thing though is to be clean. Clean hair, clean body, clean teeth, clean hands and clean finger nails. If all else fails I'm sure you have some female friends, a sister or a mate with a wife/girlfriend. It's not hard once you've asked for their help all you have to do is get dressed take your phone out and send them a photo asking their opinion. Final point in case you haven't figured out the advert's aren't true, so go easy on the body sprays.

## Should I pay, should she, do we split?

This isn't the 1950s we are no longer expected to pay for everything. Whether your date is going to expect you to pay or not though depends on her. Some women will be happy to let you pay, some will be very adamant on paying their half. Personally, I have never gone on a date without the ability to cover the costs because you never know if you'll have to or not. Before I go any further let me just state, if you pay for anything or everything it doesn't mean a woman owes you shit! I don't care if you've bought drinks, dinner, paid for the taxi and venue. You are not owed a thing! It doesn't mean you get a second date, it doesn't mean you get to fuck her. If you paid for everything and it went no further don't get shitty about it. It was on you.

So you get to the bar or the coffee shop counter order your drinks then what? I've never been bothered over the cost of a drink. I'll have a card or note ready in my hand. But if a woman wants to pay for her drink that's her choice (note some women are like this because they don't want you thinking they owe you shit. Some just know it's the 21st century). When you first meet a woman you'll know in seconds if you like her. If you like her and they are conscious about paying their half I'd say something like, "I'll get this one why don't you get the next one?" Again this is a good indicator of attraction if she agrees. She won't agree if she doesn't want to stay for another drink with you after all. Same theory can be applied to dinner, if she offers to split the bill suggest she gets it next time then you know if she's open to seeing you again. If not pay your half and don't be sensitive about it. A woman can still pay half and be interested in seeing you again after all.

If splitting a bill split it. Down the middle plain and simple that's it. Do not be the guy that gets his phone out, adds up each individual item and pays only for what they've consumed. You had a pint and she had a cocktail that cost more so what? You ordered off the set menu and she ordered from the specials board so what? This will make you look petty and she will think you're an arsehole. Doing this is the perfect way to end your date on a really shit note. You could have been perfect up until this point, but do this at the end and that's what she will remember. If money is scarce I get it, I've lived half my life counting change out of a giant vodka bottle, I really do get it. Just be honest with her beforehand and plan a date somewhere other than the place selling Wagyu steaks and Maine lobster. If she's not understanding, then forget her. She doesn't sound like a very nice person. But do not count pennies on the bill!

## Showing up with flowers or gifts

This is very simple. Don't do it. Flower's, chocolates, jewellery, etc, are for your girlfriend not your date. I know you may think you're being romantic but you're not, showing up with gifts comes across as a bribe for sex. It also comes across as desperate approval seeking behaviour. You know those shitty ad's on TV where if you buy now you get a free Parker pen? Have you ever seen one of those and thought yeah the free pen seals the deal? Of course not It's made you think hmm well that must be a shitty product to begin with. Show up with flowers you're telling her you're a shitty product.

## What should I say and do?

Well its quite simple, first of all enjoy yourself and be

yourself. Most of what I said about messaging applies here as well. As conversation goes read her bio once more have a quick glance over her messages again and make a few mental notes, other than that just go with the flow. Try not to be too serious I don't think anyone wants to discuss the merits and cons of the Tory parties manifesto on the first date. Keep it light keep it fun. Don't talk about yourself to much If she asks about you tell her, but don't say something like; "Well a little about me." Then speak your life story. This is a date not an interview. The conversation should go back and forth. Ask her questions, be interested in what she has to say and pay attention. Humour is good. If you are making her laugh then you're heading in the right direction. Note though she is a romantic interest not the lads in the pub, were looking for wit and banter between you not something that Frankie Boyle would open with. Remember your goal is to make her feel safe and comfortable in your company so that she opens up to you. Find interesting out of the box questions to get the conversation going. For example, say her profile said she really liked *Game of Thrones*. Don't just say I also like it. ask her something much more interesting, "Do you know the game Kiss Marry Kill? OK *Game of Thrones* characters, go." From there the conversation can easily deepen. "Seriously you'd marry him?" It's things like this that get humour going, that in turn relaxes you both and as easy as that you're both having a good time without even trying.

Avoid boring questions, you're learning about her not taking a witness statement. Ask then expand on the answer. If you ask her where she's from don't stop there. Where did you grow up? Oh really what was the best part of growing up down there? It's not hard to make questions more interesting and in turn make her open up to you more. If you ask about a hobby of hers don't just say, "Oh that sounds fun." Expand on it, how did you get into doing that? Do you actively compete? How often do you get to do that? What's the furthest you've ever gone? What's the highest you've ever gone? What's the craziest thing you've ever done while doing that? The more interesting you make the questions the easier it will be for you to be genuinely interested in her answers as well. (No one likes a faker) Make sure you remember the answers, because if you don't remember what she said at a later date she won't believe you were interested in what you were asking and think arsehole. If in doubt Google is again your friend. Google search, "Questions to ask a girl." About 1,760,000,000 results (0.48 seconds) There are countless lists full of interesting things to ask her. Questions she won't have been asked before and will really get her thinking. Not just about the question but about you because surely you must be an interesting guy to ask such an interesting question. Of course I have not read all these lists so scrutinise them carefully first. Just because it's on the internet does not mean it's true. If the first question on the list is, "How many drinks before you'll do anal?" Move onto the next list.

Questions like this are also a brilliant way to gauge her interest. If you ask her about her hobby let's say she rides horses for example. so you ask how she got into that and she just replies with something like, "I've always been into horses." You are getting blunt straight forward answers and it's not making it easy for you. It suggests her interest in you is not all that high. But if you then get a cute little story about how old she was when she got her first pony and what its name was she's opening up to you. This is a good sign that her interest levels are high.

Of course if you've read her bio and paid attention in the messages between you, then you should already know a few basic things about her like one or two of her interests and know you should ask questions about these. Again this is where Google can be your friend. Let's keep to the horse example you may know nothing about horses, Google does, a tiny bit of research can go a long way here. So she's just told you the cute story about her first pony, and you want to expand. Thanks to a tiny bit of research you can now ask, does she do dressage, jumping, trail hunting or play polo? Don't overdo the research though, gaining a tiny bit of knowledge to show a genuine interest and asking her better questions is good. Asking her opinion on the finer points of Spanish bloodlines or her favourite saddle maker or whatever will seem very odd if she knows you are not a horse person. Same applies to anything really.

Things not to talk about. Are the same things I told you not to say in your bio and not to say in messages, let me reiterate two things. 1.) Avoid bragging and showing off. Mention things you've done and accomplished sure, but don't brag no one likes a narcissist. 2.) Don't bring up your ex at all! I mean it, seriously think before you speak. The last thing she wants to hear is you're sat with her thinking about a different woman. Don't ask about hers either. Previous relationships are not a talking point, yours or hers.

On making her laugh. I know I said be yourself. So some of you may be thinking but my sense of humour makes Frankie Boyle look like a choir boy. Should I be myself or not? Yes of course you should always be yourself but be appropriate, when it comes to dark humour maybe don't give her both barrels right at the start. Work your way up. In 2019 I was on a date at the Edinburgh Fringe Festival. We were watching a show called *Comedy Boxing*. Two comedians competing against each other for who got the most laughs the winner then got to take a swing at the loser. They were getting the audience involved for the topics of the show. When they asked for someone famous I gave them "Jimmy Savile." Now I still maintain that I was hilarious and the stuff the comedians did with the topic was even better. My date was not amused even though she had married me fourteen month's previously and knew me well enough. She doesn't enjoy parts of my humour but we've been together for some time and she accepts them. Don't expect someone who's known you an hour or less to accept your most vile jokes. Pick the appropriate humour for the time being until you get to know each other better. Don't think of this as one of those fuck it moments I'll say it anyway and if she's offended then we wouldn't work out. It's not. While a woman's attraction to you is pretty much instant it still takes them time to warm up and open up to you before it leads to anything else. So do something stupid and she will not warm to you plain and simple.

She may test you. This has happened to all of us. Most of us were completely oblivious to it as well. I know I've failed these tests so many times. But being adaptable to change I learnt. After that I made sure I was ready for whatever could be thrown at me. Don't be offended, she isn't being a bitch, this is something that comes naturally to them. It's no different to how we naturally try to talk our way into their pants. Once you know about this it's something you can use to your advantage. This is another moment where you need to think before you speak. The right answers will maintain if not increase her attraction, the wrong answers and you could kiss goodbye to a second date. She may ask or say something intended to provoke you and see how you respond. Or say something to see how easily you'll back track or alter an opinion you've previously stated. She's testing your strength. Seeing if she can fluster you and make you lose your cool. Or seeing what you'll do if you think it will get you her approval. Again the strong response is the winner. Remember everything I've said so far, a secure and confident man won't lose his cool. He won't get defensive, he will remain unfazed there should be nothing she can throw at you that you cannot handle.

I went out with a girl once who tested me like no other, here are some of the things she threw at me. She asked me how long I'd been on the website for? I said about seven months and without missing a beat she looked me dead in the eye and said, "Wow seven months So am I sat having lunch with a player or a loser who can't close a deal?" A weak response would have been to become defensive and say something like "No, no, I'm not a player I swear. I'm not a loser though I can close a deal." Give her an answer like that she has the upper hand and starts losing respect for you. Instead I smirked, looked amused and said, "Perhaps I haven't met a woman exceptional enough to make me want to delete my account yet." There may have been a better response I could have used. But I stayed cool, deflected with humour and she didn't get under my skin. Test passed.

After lunch we got a drink. Stood at the bar she ordered a gin and tonic and I ordered a beer. Again without missing a beat she turned to me struck an aggressive pose and said, "Urgh you're not ordering beer? It's so boring, only boring people drink beer, why don't you order something more interesting?" At this point she was trying to see if she could make me backtrack. See if I was weak enough to change my order thinking it would get her approval. The barman at this point stopped dead in his tracks. Again I smirked, looked over at him and said, "beer please." He poured my beer. With a smile I took it from the bar had a sip while looking at her placed it back down and said, "Well clearly you haven't gone out with the right beer drinker." She still wasn't done. As we sat down at a table she asked, "Why did you order a half, What man orders halves?" Again I smiled and said, "A man with a full evening planned. I'm saving space for later on." Each time I kept cool made her think she was amusing me, deflected with humour and passed her testing. On the last one I also gave her the impression that I've been telling you to give. That I was a high value individual with an interesting life. I didn't say what I was doing, was I out with friends, did I have another date? I left that blank for her mind to make up. After that I turned it on her and asked, "So as there is a trace amount of beer on my lips if I were to kiss you goodbye will you think it's a boring kiss?" I kissed her goodbye and went home, my phone went off on the drive back. She text me saying what a great time she had and wanted to know when I could see her again.

These are just a few examples. Google search, "Women testing men," read everything you can and watch the YouTube video's. It will pay off. Think of this as just evening the playing field. It's never been any secret to women that we're trying to talk our way into their pants. They've known what we were doing all along and could act accordingly. Most of us have been oblivious to them testing us our entire lives. Don't think of it as an unfair advantage. After all if she likes you she wants you to pass these tests right?

Meeting a nervous or shy woman. When you go on

a date with a woman and she's clearly nervous or shy what should you do? The answer is pretty much the same as before, make them feel safe and comfortable make them laugh. Conversation can be a little trickier, there may be some awkward silences and you may need to adjust your humour a little. My standard sense of humour is to take the piss. Not in a nasty way but if I met someone who was very shy I'd lay off that. I don't want to be putting them down and potentially forcing them back further into their shell. For example I once said to a girl, "wow you're so chatty tonight I can hardly get a word in edge ways." I was trying to make her laugh but it was a mistake. One I learnt from. Ask them the right questions, show an interest it really isn't that different. The only thing you need to pay attention to is are they shy or just not interested? Because the signals they send out can look very similar. A shy person might not want to make eye contact and will be looking everywhere around the room except you. Someone who's disinterested may do the same it can be hard to tell. Smart phones make figuring this out a little easier though. Generally the shy woman will be looking around the room the disinterested bored woman will be glued to her phone.

Should I compliment her? Simply put if you like her, the way she looks, what she's wearing and you want to then yes. Most women put effort in their appearance and like to know it's been noticed or is appreciated. But don't go overboard. There's a difference between giving a girl a compliment and kissing her arse, don't do the latter. Like I've said before if she's beautiful she's well aware of that already, you spewing out words to that effect every five minutes will do nothing but come across as weak and seeking her approval. So be original and don't go over the top with it.

The alarm bells and warning signs I went over in the previous chapter will be more evident and easier to spot in person so look out for anything she says or does that sets them off. There are also other red flags to look out for in person. See below.

## Red flags in person

So there are hundreds of these and of course what might be a red flag for me may not be a red flag for you but something's you need to be very aware of. The red flags I'm going to go over here are things to look out for in the initial meeting and early dating stages. There are more red flags to look out for in the relationship stage as well. This is an area I've learnt the hard way, as I've already said don't be like I used to be. Don't be so blinded by a woman willing to date you that you fail to notice she is all kinds of wrong for you. So for the first date especially and the next few that follow on keep your eyes open.

## She can't put her phone down

Now a sensible woman may have a friend she needs to let know she is OK upon meeting you, that's just common sense and a good idea, I know I've told several female friends in the past if they get a bad feeling they just need to text me and I'll drop whatever I'm doing to come and get them. You're still a stranger from the internet. If a woman texts a friend to let them know she's OK don't get offended or act insulted about it, if you get funny about it then it implies you're the reason she needs a friend to know where she is in the first place. However if after that she can't stay off her phone it raises a red flag to me. To me it says she's rude, uninterested or both. If she cannot disconnect from her phone for a couple of hours when meeting you then is she worth your time? I'm not saying have nothing to do with her if she gets a call and has to take it. But do you want to bother with someone who was more interested in Instagram or Snapchat the entire time she was sat across from you? Side note: if she takes hours to reply to your messages but then spends all her time with you on her phone do the maths!

## She's overly judgemental of material things

Signs of a gold digger or very shallow individual. Of course we all judge people and make assumptions based on peoples possessions it can't be helped. Their possessions are part of their appearance and judging someone's appearance is the initial part of attraction after all. It's also only natural for a woman to be attracted to a successful man and nice possessions are a sign of success. Look out for someone who's overly judgemental of certain things though. Is she overly interested in which car in the car park is yours? Is she judgemental that yours is the Ford and not the BMW? As the old saying goes you get what you pay for. We all know cheap stuff isn't cool and cool stuff isn't cheap but know where your line is drawn. If you're anything like me you wouldn't dream of paying over £100 for a pair of jeans just because they have a brand name sewn onto them. Same for trainers I'm not a professional athlete so I see no sense in paying over three figures for a pair of them. My £50 watch keeps time just as well as one that costs thousands. If your date is overly judgemental or unimpressed by something like this, then she may be too materialistic for you, a gold digger or very shallow.

If you meet someone like this and they are judgemental of you or your possessions don't stand for it. Don't let them put you down, don't let them make you feel bad, this is their failing not yours. She isn't better than you, she has no right to make you feel any different. Under no circumstances think you need to change or buy expensive shit to earn her approval! She isn't the one for you, move on. If she walks away from you for the same reasons she has done you a favour.

Of course if you do Drive a high-end car, wear expensive clothes and your watch is worth more than my annual salary you may see things differently. If these things are important to you maybe someone who's not remotely interested or impressed by them isn't the right one for you either.

On a side note materialism is a classic sign of insecurity. If she's very materialistic keep both eyes open. Some of the worst people I've ever met have tried to hide it with material possessions. They need the car, the expensive watch, the designer clothes because they are nothing without them. They try to use these things to hide what's beneath, the fact they are empty within.

## She brings up her ex, ex's or keeps putting them down

If her ex comes up at all during the first date be very careful, big red flag! If her ex keeps popping up in conversation guess what, she may be out with you but she's thinking about him. Loosely translated this means she would probably prefer to be there with him instead of you. Meaning she isn't over him and she's a potential flight risk. Do you want to date someone knowing you're giving her your full attention but there's a different guy in her head? I know I wouldn't.

She won't sit there and say something like, "Oh me and my ex used to come here, it was great, we always sat over there I really miss him. I wonder what he's doing right now maybe he's thinking of me too?" You need to be able to tell the difference here between what she says and what she means. It will be far more subtle, his name will occasionally come up, usually when it had no place in the conversation.

Once after food shopping I was waiting for a pizza with a girl I was dating, as we sat there out the blue she said, "You know it's strange I haven't run into 'Insert name' at all. You think we would have by now in the supermarket or just in the general area."

Considering the discussion up until that point had been about what movie should we watch when we get home I thought where the hell did that come from? She then spent the journey home trying to convince me she didn't miss him, was over him and wasn't thinking about him at all. Not sure who she was trying to convince more me or her? (literal translation she couldn't stop thinking about him but didn't want me knowing that.)

The next night while washing up after dinner she brought him up in conversation again. I was taller and leaner he was shorter and stockier. Somehow she got onto the topic and began telling me she didn't want me feeling insecure because his arms were much bigger than mine and then promised me it didn't bother her (I hadn't asked if it bothered her, I remember thinking well that had never crossed my mind until now, thanks for that. now I know it's crossed your mind and it bothers you). Remember I said in Chapter 5 how women on the rebound tend to go for the polar opposite of their ex. That's when it dawned on me I was the rebound! From there it all started to go south. I wanted to trust her but part of me just couldn't because I knew her feelings were mixed up. Needless to say a few weeks later I received a very emotional phone call from her late at night because she had let him back into her life. Trust me gentlemen it is not worth the aggro.

If she keeps insulting her ex's or putting them down. What does this say about her? That she's a really shitty judge of character that makes poor choices, or they couldn't all be the problem and she was? Maybe both?

When I was much younger I worked in the leisure industry. The majority of staff in the leisure industry are all in their late teens and early 20's. So a large mixed group of young fit people full of hormones and still fairly new to alcohol. You can guess what it was like on weekends, after hours and when they threw staff parties. Forget love triangles we had love dodecahedron's going on, everyone had dated everyone. I became close friends with a girl (just friends) for about a year. I heard horror story after horror story about all her ex's and I can remember thinking things like how could he be so awful to her? Why would he say or do that? Oh poor her, I'd never treat a girlfriend like that. Eventually one thing lead to another and I became her boyfriend. Everyone said what a great couple we would make as we were already best friends and I believed them. I wouldn't do any of those terrible things the previous ones had. Within a couple of months though it became very apparent all the problems she had in the past were not just the ex's fault. Some of the horror stories she had told me suddenly became quite relatable from the males points of view. Fast forward another month and I had joined the rank of her ex's and she was telling someone else horror stories about me. I had never been anything but decent to her the fact was she was just difficult.

Moral of the story. If she has nothing but bad things to say about all her ex's maybe, just maybe, it wasn't just their fault, maybe she is the problem but is unable to accept responsibility for her failings.

## Rudeness and being mean

You'll learn a lot about a person's qualities or lack of by how they treat others so pay attention it's a good indicator on how she may treat you in the future. Learn the difference between teasing, banter and outright meanness as well. Teasing you and being playful is one thing but don't get it confused with her being outright nasty towards you. Some people are just horrible. WALK AWAY. Others may be doing it to manipulate you. Put you down to lower your self-esteem and make you try to seek their approval. Don't fall for it, if you do it's a downwards spiral and it will continually get worse.

## Overreactions

This can be a tricky one to judge. We have all had a girlfriend in the past seemingly lose their shit with us over something we consider trivial and insignificant, usually because there is a deeper core issue we have failed to pick up on. I'm not going into the finer details of that though. I'm talking in the dating stage. Here an overreaction is an overreaction plain and simple. Has she chewed out the bartender because she said no ice in her drink? Has she wanted to claw another woman's eyes out because she accidentally bumped into her? Has she lost it with you because you smiled at the waitress? Dating is supposed to be fun, how can going out with someone like this be fun? If someone exhibits behaviour like this don't go out with them again you're not dating, you're playing Russian roulette.

It's not necessarily aggressive over reactions either. It can be about anything. Other examples I can give you from personal experience are a girl once ruined an evening by sulking the entire time. Her reason the dessert shop we were going to go to at the end of the evening had shut unexpectedly due to a staff shortage. A fully grown woman ruining an entire evening because we couldn't go to Cream's at the end of the night was ridiculous. The same woman once ruined a day out sulking because the day we went to the beach it was overcast instead of sunny.

Behaviour like this is a sign of emotional immaturity, being excessively spoilt as a child and receiving a lack of discipline growing up. Dating someone like this is exhausting and not remotely fun. It's just not worth your time.

## Deceitfulness and lying

Is she coming out with things that just don't sound right? Is her body language suggesting she's lying? We will all embellish a little when meeting someone, we don't want to sound boring but watch out for dishonesty. You may think it's harmless white lies but if she's lying to you from day one where does it lead if you keep dating? Dishonest people cannot be trusted. Worst case scenario this is someone who will cheat on you if you end up in a relationship. Best case scenario this is the type of person who will lie to you and say what you want to hear in order to impress you. If it leads to a relationship you find out half of it has been built on lies and you're not a good match. We've all been there before right? When you first meet her she just loves all the same things, you think great. Then further down the road you suggest going and doing one of these things only to find she lied to you and she would rather watch paint dry.

## Is she getting things mixed up?

Is she confusing things between you and someone else? For example say you hate football and she knows this. Then she says to you, "So did you watch the match last night, I saw the final score on the news this morning your prediction was correct." She's getting her wires crossed between you and other men she's talking to or seeing. Let me reiterate she is doing nothing wrong by talking to or dating other men. You owe each other nothing in the early stages of dating. Also if you're going to get shitty and be insecure about the possibility of her also seeing other men it doesn't tell her you're the top choice when she decides to pick one of you. The red flag to watch out for is if her words don't match up with her actions. Is she saying she's only seeing you, or she wants a relationship and commitment but still confusing you with others and getting what she says mixed up? It's another sign of a dishonest or insincere woman.

## Poor timekeeping

This can be tricky to pick up on when initially dating. Traffic can be bad, public transport can run behind etc. But someone who is constantly late to me is waving a big red flag. I'm not talking five to ten minutes here or there, we know getting ready is much more complicated for a woman and takes longer I accept that, I'm talking about someone who is constantly late to the point they have no respect for your time and they are happy to waste it. Maybe you believe in reincarnation or an afterlife? Personally, I believe we get one go at this so time is precious. Therefore my time is the greatest gift I can give. People willing to waste my time don't deserve me sharing it with them plain and simple. Several years ago I had a girlfriend who did just this. We would arrange to go out and a time I'd be at hers to pick her up. When I'd get there she would never be ready. Most of the time she wouldn't even be dressed. When I'd suggest she started getting ready as we had somewhere to be, she would be very nonchalant about it and respond saying things like, "let me just see the end of the show I'm watching," or something else like that. I used to make excuses for her, say things like she's just one of those people who'll be late to her own funeral. But the truth is she simply had no respect for me or my time. If you know what your time is worth do not put up with someone wasting it.

Now you're both there in person it is much easier for you to judge her interest and attraction in you. If you're clueless to female body language YouTube has the answers for you. Learn it, she will not look you in the eye and say I really like you and I want you to kiss me. But if she wants you to, her non-verbal communication will be screaming it! Is she smiling, laughing, making eye contact, is she touching her hair or neck? Does she lean in when talking? Is she touching your hand or arm when she talks to you? These are all things to look out for. Get on YouTube watch videos and see it done, so you know exactly what you are looking for.

What should you do? First of all don't be late. I know life happens, traffic is unpredictable sometimes it cannot be helped. If this happens call ahead let them know, good manners cost nothing. If you arrive first so you are seated when she arrives, don't stay seated, stand up to greet her. When you greet her don't shake her hand, you shake her father's hand if you get that far, not hers. I prefer to greet a woman with a hug and a kiss on the cheek. After all you're on a date as potential romantic interests. Note I said prefer though. As you greet a woman watch her body language act accordingly, the last thing you want to do is something they won't be comfortable with. If you're unsure ask before the date, but ask the right way. Asking the wrong way says you're unsure and lack confidence. I have text women before a date and said, "So how do you want to handle the greeting? Stand six feet apart awkwardly shuffle our feet and mumble it's nice to meet you? The overly formal handshake? Or can I give you a hug? We can throw in the additional cheek kiss as well. I'll try my best not to bang heads with you as I lean down." Something like that isn't asking too seriously. It's funny, I've always got a response like "a hug is fine" or "surprise me."

Put your phone on silent and keep it in your pocket. You're there to meet her not ignore her. If you are going to be showing her something on your phone make sure you've logged out of any dating apps and muted your messaging notifications. If she's looking at a photo you don't want a dating site saying you have new messages while it's in her hand.

Don't check out other women in her company. You didn't get away with it, she sees it. Watch out for overly flirtatious servers. Both male and female. Sometimes you'll be on a first date and the server is behaving like you're a celebrity she's had a crush on for years. Be polite but don't buy into it, they're fucking with you. In turn if the server is male and doing it to your date don't get upset about it. You'll only look weak or insecure. Laugh about it, find it amusing, it can give the two of you something else to talk and laugh about. My theory is like most of us some of them like to have a little fun at work from time to time. When you're on a first date some people can just tell. Especially servers they see it all the time, you two are clearly giving off first date vibes, and they want to have some fun at your expense. I really want to ask servers about this one day but now I'm married it just doesn't happen anymore.

If someone comes on to your date, don't get angry or defensive. But don't become submissive and back away from it either. Behaving like that makes you look scared, it actually makes the other guy look attractive because you appear threatened by it. If another man is checking out your date take pride in it. Yes she is a beautiful woman and yes she is here with me. Be secure not weak. If someone actually comes on to her and is flirting be amused, give off the impression that you're totally confident she won't find better than you. I had a drunken idiot come over to my table once trying to convince my girlfriend to get up and dance with him. What did I do? I leaned back and said, "Well I don't know babe do you think you can keep up with him? He looks very light on his feet." If I had gotten pissed off I would have validated him looked jealous and weak. Instead I gave off the vibe that I was not phased because I knew 100% she was coming home with me.

Don't be rude. Not to her or anyone else. I shouldn't even have to explain this, just don't be rude it's not difficult. Be a decent person not an arsehole. Short of whipping your dick out, pissing in her face while simultaneously calling her mother an anal loving slut and her father a paedophile rudeness is the biggest self-sabotage you can do! Graphic image right? It's there to get the point across don't be rude. Some men try to big themselves up by belittling others. Don't try to do this to impress a woman, don't do it at all. It doesn't make you look strong it makes you look like a bully. If you want to appear strong then be a strong person, don't attempt it at the expense of others. When you date someone she will learn a lot about you by how you treat people. In particular those in the service industry, so bartenders, servers, cab drivers, door staff and bouncers. Literally all the people you are going to encounter while dating. If you're rude and disrespectful to them, it tells this woman that's likely how she will be treated by you later on in the relationship. It's a massive turnoff. Putting women aside for a minute if you're like this anyway you shouldn't be, sort your life out. Become a decent human! I've said it already the world is harsh enough as it is. Don't add to it! If it's still not clear let me offer an example. You're having a dinner date. Your server brings you your meal and it's incorrect. You ordered rare steak but you got well done or whatever. Accepting what you haven't ordered and eating it anyway is weak behaviour. Calling the server over to correct it is good. Speaking and treating them like a piece of shit because of it is not good. It doesn't make you look strong or impress anyone it makes you look like an arsehole. Don't be an arsehole, don't be rude be a decent human being.

Be aware of your subconscious movements. Don't suddenly realise you've been sat there in front of her scratching your arse or with your finger up your nose for several minutes. Don't show up drunk, don't end up drunk either. Over all if you have common sense use it. But remember have a good time. If you're not doing that then what's the point?

Know when to end it. Don't let a date drag on until you've both run out of things to say and it's dead. You want to finish the date on a high note, Think the boxer who retires undefeated in his prime, not the one who continues until he's broken. You need to end the date while it's going well so it leads to a second date. Once you've left each other's company you want her to get home and think what a great time. Not well it seemed good at first but got a bit awkward and weird towards the end, know when to call it a day. Remember always leave them wanting more. I'm not saying you rush off but when the food is finished or the drinks are done. Just end the date before the conversation is done as well, don't loiter unnecessarily. It makes you look very unsure of yourself. Remember you're a confident guy. You should be decisive and have no problem making the decision to call it a night. Take charge It's simple enough, "OK shall we make a move?" Once outside assuming she drove there ask her "Where are you parked? I'll walk you to your car." Don't ask "Would you like me to walk you to your car?" You'll sound unsure, you should be sure of yourself. If all has gone well, you have her attraction and her interest she will be happy to have you walk her to her car. If you've read it wrong she may decline, or she left long before.

## The goodbye kiss

Goodbye kiss not a goodbye handshake. If she's offering you her hand it's a no. How do you know if she wants to kiss you? Well you're the one on the date, not me, hopefully you've read the signs right. If you go to kiss her and she pulls away or turns so you get her cheek. She didn't want to kiss you.

(remember the rules don't get shitty about it, she's not the one for you or it was a bit too soon for her)

These are the tell-tale signs she does not want to kiss you:

- She declines you walking her to her car.
- She keeps a distance between the two of you as she says goodbye.
- She doesn't linger and goes to leave swiftly.
- The body language covered earlier is non-existent.
- She turns away.
- She says no.

Only do it if you actually want to kiss her. Did you enjoy yourself, do you want to see her again do you like her? If the answer's no, don't kiss her. You're not obligated to and you shouldn't lead someone on. If you kiss her on the cheek, you may think you're being a gentleman but it's also a mixed signal, that's how you say goodbye to female friends.

The tell-tale signs she wants to kiss you.

- All the body language and signs have been right. They're still present as you're saying goodbye.

- She lingers (for example she's stood there with her car keys in her hand. If she wasn't keen she would have unlocked it climbed in and shut the door).

- She is close to you, she doesn't step back if you step forward.

- She asks for a lift home. Trust me no woman wants to get in your car or wants you knowing where their home is if they are not interested.

- She kisses you first. (sometimes it happens).


If you're really clueless you can always just ask her. Though this isn't the best advice, but if you're worried you're reading it wrong it's better than a missed opportunity. What's the worst that can happen? She says no, then you know and it's not like you have to see her again. I've done this a few times for varying reasons. I haven't been sure, or the girl I was dating seemed quite shy. Again if you do this only ask if you think it's a yes, if you think it's a no it's definitely a no. (If it's a no don't get shitty) Don't actually ask her, "Can I kiss you?" Let me make that perfectly clear don't do that! Eliminate as many variables as possible to reduce your chances of getting it wrong. She's lingering, good, she hasn't run away, good, she's close, good. If you're still unsure give her a hug and before you let go say something like, "I really want to kiss you," or "I'd love a kiss before I go." Don't ask can I kiss you?

I went on a date with a girl and it was her first time meeting someone from a dating site. I liked her right away and she was showing all the right signs. However as this was her first time she was also quite nervous. So when we said goodbye she gave me a nervous hug. As she went to pull away I held on looked in her eyes, "I want to kiss you" She smiled and looked keen but said no. But she didn't let go of me either. So I asked her "Don't you want to?" She said she did, So I asked her, "Then what's the problem?" Before I finished the sentence her lips were on mine. We kissed then she giggled and ran off. We were together for nearly two years.

It's a goodbye kiss only. Hint is in the title "goodbye!" Now you've kissed her goodbye it's time to say goodbye. Thank her for a great time, say you had fun say it was great meeting her, whatever you like, then leave. Don't push your luck and try to go any further. More than once I've had a woman tell me they were really impressed I didn't try to have sex with them on a first date. Remember the stunning Polish girl I mentioned before? We had sex on our second date. Her exact words were I really impressed her by not trying it on the first date when I dropped her off home. If I had tried it she would have made me wait over a month. So don't push your luck. You've both had a good time, you've both willingly kissed, a second date seems like a sure thing this is the way to ruin that.

For example someone I know from my home town once set up a date online with a girl he knew of. We all went to the same school but different years. She was apparently quite well known for one-night stands. The date went well but all went to shit at the end when it didn't lead to sex. He couldn't understand why. I remember asking him, "Did you not think she was on that site because she wanted to meet someone to date not fuck? If that's all she wanted she would have been back in the bars and clubs not online. You read it wrong, treated her wrong and now you've ruined what could have been a sure thing in a week or two." He was wrong he was not honest with her about his intentions from the beginning. Still it's a good example of how it will ruin things even with someone who has a "reputation" for being easy.

Of course if a woman invites you back or suggests you take her to your place and wants to have sex then it's down to you. Last time this happened to me I turned her down (I'm not saying if this comes up you should do that it's your choice.) She was in disbelief, she had never been turned down before.

If anything it worked in my favour what she couldn't have she wanted even more. I think turning her down did only good things because when we did have sex it was definitely worth it (Note I turned her down in a polite and playful manner that let her know I wanted to. I didn't look at her appalled and say NO!).

# CHAPTER 7

# After the date

So the date is over and you've gone home now what? My advice be happy, sit down relax, read, turn on the TV, flog yourself with a spiked chain, do whatever it is you normally do to chill out. But be happy because this was a success. Regardless of outcome. You messaged someone online and it resulted in you two meeting. You had your first date. That's a win whatever way you look at it. DO NOT message or call her as soon as you get home. If a man does it, it suggests he is clingy or needy. Unattractive qualities you definitely don't want to show right after the first date. If a woman calls or messages you almost right away though well done she is showing a high level of attraction (Unless of course the message is saying never contact me again you freak! If you get that message return to page one, let's start again).

I've seen female friends after a good date look at their phone and be sad the guy hasn't messaged them. I've seen the same female friends after a good first date get put off because the guy has messaged them. All of a sudden they have gone from, "We hit it off" to "Urgh he won't leave me alone." I suggest you give it two or three days and see if she messages or calls you first if she does use that as the opening to set up a second date. If she doesn't and you want to see her again then contact her.

## If it didn't go well

It happens, everyone isn't right for everyone. It's just the way it is. Sometimes you'll both leave a date clearly thinking well thank God that's over, as you both knew there was nothing there. Other times you might be into her but she's not into you or vice versa. You might get ghosted, or you might get a message saying something like, "Hey it was really nice meeting you last night but there just wasn't any spark there for me," or, "I don't think you're what I'm looking for." If this happens be polite the same rules all still apply. "Hi, it was very nice meeting you too, good luck I hope you find who you're looking for." Then don't contact her again. Don't ask or demand to know why, don't ask for a second chance. Attraction is not a choice. If she didn't like you, you won't talk her into it or change her mind, it's either there or it's not (this is another area where movies and TV have lied to you. In the movies the guy refuses to give up on love and the woman eventually realises "the one" has been there in front of her the whole time. In real life refusing to give up results in being blocked or a visit from the police). Remain polite though because as I said women talk. You might be messaging a friend of hers in three weeks and she finds out. She could tell her friend, "Oh I know him, real genuine guy," or "stay away he called me a cunt or stalked me when I didn't want to go out with him again."

Sometimes attraction just isn't there, and you may not understand why. In 2012 I messaged a girl and instantly we clicked. We had great conversation and set up a date midweek. Things were going so well she told me her house mate was away on the weekend and insinuated I should stay over providing the first date went well. When we met in person it just fell flat on its face. It was as if we both had our personality's sucked out of us when we came within range of one another. Yes she was very pretty, but I was not remotely attracted to her, nor her towards me. We had a very boring date and said goodbye. Needless to say we didn't spend the weekend together. About two months later she messaged me again on the dating site asking how I'd been and if I'd had any luck? I replied saying something like, probably as much luck as you if you've resorted to messaging me again. We started talking and the conversation was fantastic. I asked if she wanted to go grab a drink and play some pool? I could do with getting out of the house. An hour later there we were, our personality's both removed not enjoying each other's company. I literally remember saying to her, "I don't get it, messaging were great and physically you really do it for me but we meet and I don't know what the hell this is." She said she was thinking exactly the same thing. We said our goodbyes and that was that. If attraction's not there then it's not there. Nothing can change that and it doesn't always make sense.

Occasionally it might be the other way round. The woman may be into you but you're just not into her. I advocate against ghosting. Personally, I think it's cowardly. Don't string her along it's very unfair just be honest and tell her there wasn't anything there for you wish her luck and move on. She may not like it but she will respect you for it. On the off chance she doesn't like or won't accept your answer that's when you can ghost her. This is one of the other reasons I like to keep social media and dating separate until established.

Can we just be friends? You might get asked something like this, usually following a date or a couple of them you get a message that reads along the lines of, "I really like you and I think you're a great guy but I just don't see you like that, can we be friends?" Now this is the time for being honest. So many men will automatically say, "Yes of course" because they don't want to seem like an arsehole, or they think being her friend means they're on the first rung of the ladder, she will come around and they will soon start climbing. (You won't!) If you actually become friends the attraction's not there for her. Being her friend and doing all the things a boyfriend should do for her without the intimacy will not make her see you in a new light and realise she was mistaken. She will be oblivious or choose to ignore the fact that you want her, you will become more and more frustrated until you actively resent her for it. Leading to you losing your cool and calling her up late at night upset, demanding to know why she doesn't like you like that.

She was not on a dating site looking for friends. If she only wants to be your friend it means one of two things. 1.) she didn't have it in her to ghost you or just say no. So she suggested you just be friends. So interpret it as it is, she's not interested! It does not mean put in more work and you'll get there in the end. 2.) you did something wrong. Things were probably going well her attraction and interest was there or getting there, but you did something to turn her off. This usually happens after a few dates, things seem good but then she just wants to be friends. Again read it for what it is You messed up somewhere she's no longer interested.

So be completely honest with her, "Hey I've had a great time going out with you as well but I have no interest in a platonic friendship with you. Good luck finding what you're looking for if anything changes you have my number." Unless you genuinely only want to be her friend and have no other desires on her don't agree to it. It leads to nothing but sorrow (yes I'd love to meet you once a month, buy you lunch and listen to you bitch about the latest guy to fuck you over while my inner monologue screams YOU SHOULD BE WITH ME). That sound like a fun friendship to you? Because it doesn't to me. If she suddenly only wants to be friends the chances are you did something weak that turned her off and caused her attraction levels to drop. She may now be testing you, saying, "I'd love to just be friends," is another weak response and failing that test. The response I gave above is a much stronger answer and may even cause her attraction levels to raise slightly. She may think, "Oh okay he's not the pushover I thought he was," and that was all that was needed. Either way, show her you have a backbone it's better than the alternative.

It went really well, she got in contact with you after,

but you still ended up getting ghosted. Sometimes this happens, you had a great date, all went well, you both wanted to see each other again she contacts you after, then she vanishes. It might happen after one date it might happen after three or five. Don't read too much into it. Most of the time it's nothing to do with you. Like I've said before you don't know a woman's state of mind going into things, or where her life's at. She probably did have a great first date with you, but the next day might have had a great fourth date with someone else and they have decided to get together. After your good date she might have had an awful date with someone else. Bad enough to put her off everyone and everything for a while. It could be something really trivial like she discovered you and her cousin were a couple in year eleven. There are a million other possibilities but I only have so much ink. The answer remains the same get over it, learn and move on.

## It did go well

Great but remember what I said about jumping the gun and coming on too strong. If all went well and you kissed goodbye you know you're into each other. Don't message or call her right away. Like I said give it a couple of days and see if she contacts you first. It's a good indicator of just how high her interest is. If she contacts you then it's the perfect opportunity to set up a second date. She may even get in contact asking you out. If that happens then you know she's interested. If she doesn't contact you after a couple of days then contact her. If she didn't contact you it doesn't necessarily mean she's uninterested, she might have just been unsure if she should contact you first or not. By waiting a couple of days you've given her the opportunity to wonder and a chance to think about you. You've given her enough time to want you to call her.

So contact her, same rules apply. The point of this is to get a date not become her BFF and stay on the phone all evening. Don't be a robot make a date and hang up, ask how her weeks going etc, etc, but try to limit phone calls to about ten minutes no more than 15. You still need some mystery, intrigue and something to talk about in person. If you're texting instead of calling don't get caught up in an endless message chain. Ask her out the same way as before, "When are you free to meet up again?" Don't ask specific days you still don't know her schedule. Again don't ask if she's free but when, sound confident. Once you've arranged a second date same as before, back off. Staying in contact is fine but the ultimate aim is to meet up, and get close. Not become kindred spirits through a tiny screen in your hands. Remember get a date not a pen pal.

# CHAPTER 8

# Your second date and more

Once I've started dating someone, by that I mean it's gone past the first date and were now communicating via phone instead of the dating site. I will go online go into the settings and block the woman from seeing my online status on the dating site. For those who are unfamiliar with this. It's a feature where you can block certain accounts from seeing you online or from seeing your account at all. Usually reserved for women to stop creepy men from stalking them. I do this so she cannot see when I'm online, and also so I cannot see when she is online. Like I said neither of us are doing anything wrong by talking or setting up dates with other people. Neither of us have made any promises. But it can lead to awkward conversation if she utters the words, "So I saw you online last night," this is a simple fix. Be honest you don't want to see someone you're dating online knowing she's talking to other men either. I've told you not to be petty or insecure, this will help you do that.

## Planning your second date

Needless to say the second date should be a bit more interesting than a pub or coffee shop. Look for something entertaining but inexpensive you want the give off the message you're looking to spend time with her not impress her with lavish places. You still want places you can talk and get to know each other more, so for now avoid cinema's, concerts and other similar venue's. If you can find something that you both share a common interest in even better. If you can't think of a good idea then you're not trying hard enough, it's not rocket science. Go bowling, shoot some pool, go to a country park, hire some Segways. If you both like history go to the National Trust website and find somewhere. If you're both cyclists suggest a good route you know with great views and places to stop for refreshments. If you both have horses go hacking. If you're both really into art find an independent gallery. If you're both keen photographers tell her you were thinking of going somewhere to photograph it's landscape or it's wildlife or it's decay or whatever terminology you use and see if she would like to join you. If you can do something that comes naturally to both of you great you'll feel relaxed and the conversation will be effortless. At this point though do not ask her what she wants to do for a second date. You should have been paying enough attention in the first one to pick something she will agree too. Remember, be decisive.

## Meeting her there or picking her up?

Well there's no hard and fast rule, it depends on several variables. However if you offer to pick her up and she declines remember the rules. Don't get shitty and respect her boundaries. If you do pick her up make sure your car is clean. I'm not saying you need to get it professionally valeted that morning but at least remove the old McDonald's wrappers, parking tickets, whatever's been rattling round in the back for the past month and bang off the floor mats. Also you may have gone nose blind. An air freshener cannot hurt. It's not so much what car you show up in that's important (again if it is that important to her she may not be the one for you). But how you treat that car. If it looks like a landfill inside and smells no better What do you think that suggests about you? It suggests you don't take care of your home or yourself very well either.

Personally, I won't offer to pick a woman up unless I am confident she will accept. So usually I'll leave it till the third date unless she asks of course. If you do pick her up don't just text her saying I'm outside and stay in the car. She may not want you coming to the front door for whatever reason. Nosy housemates or parent's but at the very least get out of your car and greet her properly. If you kissed her goodbye last time, be confident and kiss her when you say hello as well, be a gentleman and open the door for her, it will probably catch her by surprise. If you meet her at location the same applies if you kissed her goodbye on your first date you kiss her hello on your next one.

## The testing may now start or continue

Now you're not strangers, certain things like conversation should be much easier. Now that she's more comfortable with you though this is also the time you're more likely to be tested, she will want to see what you're made of, (sad news guys the testing never stops not even after "I do"). So keep yourself composed and don't let her knock you off your centre. This is why I've been advocating improving yourself, fixing your minor flaws, having confidence self-worth and seeing yourself as a high value individual from the beginning. You don't pass a woman's testing in the early stages then it's all over. If a woman thinks you're weak she will test you at any time, if your response is weak she will keep testing you. It's not enough to expect it and have a few strong witty responses ready. You have to be strong and stay that way. That means having self-worth and seeing yourself as a high value individual. Remember if you don't think and believe it no one else will.

## Why do they test us?

In essence they want to see what you're made of and figure out what kind of man you are. If the concept of a woman testing is new to you, you probably don't like the idea of it very much. I know at face value it can seem devious, bitchy and a lot like they're playing mind games. Why can't they just ask or communicate in a normal fashion? The simple answer is because you may say one thing with your words but an entirely different thing with your behaviour. If you've told her you don't let anyone push you around and you don't care about the opinions of others. But then when she disagrees with something you change your opinion or take back what you said earlier to align with her views thinking you'll get her approval she knows she's dealing with a weak man. If she says something provocative to you and you get angry she knows she's dealing with someone who has a lack of self-control.

Let's be honest here. Would you tell her, "I have low self-esteem, I can't stand up to my boss, I bottle all this up until I can't take it anymore then I snap and make an arse of myself?" Would you admit you were a manipulative man who intended to use her, or a violent man who intends to hurt her? Of course you wouldn't. As I've said earlier don't take it personally it comes naturally to them she isn't intentionally being a bitch towards you. She's just trying to figure out what kind of man you are.

She may now start to ask you more serious questions depending how comfortable she feels with you. Anything from are you dating anyone else? To how many sexual partners have you had? Be prepared for anything. Don't get defensive you are not guilty of anything after all. Keep it light don't become serious. Answering questions like this usually leads to nowhere good. But outright refusing to answer them can sound worse. You may be wondering why is she asking me things like this after I have explicitly told you to avoid asking a woman questions like this from the beginning. She may be testing you, she may be clueless as to what is or what's not appropriate to ask. Either way if these sort of questions get asked you had best know how to respond. Remaining cool, calm and using humour is the best way to deal with it in my experience. If a woman was to ask me am I dating anyone else? I'd look at her and say something like, "No it's only me and you sat at this table." I would keep to that kind of response. If she responded saying something like that's not what I meant I'd reply asking, "Well what exactly did you mean?" If she asked if I was seeing anyone else I'd say something like, "well there are people on the tables behind you that I can see but all my attention is focused on you." I would try to keep it as playful as possible. If she started to get annoyed about it I wouldn't stop being playful about it either. I'd ask her, "What's the matter? I'm here with you aren't I? Why would you concern yourself with anyone else when I'm here with you?"

If I was also dating another woman or women I'm not technically lying to her because I don't want to do that. But by being playful with my answer I've given her the impression I might be. At this point if we were only on our second date I wouldn't be doing anything wrong if I was and believe it or not if she thinks you have options because you're a high value desirable guy, her interest level is likely to rise. Scientific studies have found men are more attractive when desired by other women.

Other questions like how many sexual partners have you had only lead to issues if asked early on. It's a serious question and discussion to be had with someone once you are in a committed relationship sure, but while dating no. You know how I said to expand on questions. Well can you imagine trying to expand on this so how many? Wow that many? Did you know their names? How many one-night stands? Catch anything nasty? Learn anything kinky off the German au-pair? It's not a topic for dating, you answer a question like this it will probably kill the conversation and make it awkward. Unless of course you and your date have matched up because you're a pair of sex addicts and literally cannot get enough. Again I'd keep any response light and say something like, "Well I don't kiss and tell, especially not on the second date."

## The actual date

When it comes to the actual date, most of the same advice still applies. Especially when it comes to dressing yourself and what not to do or say. If you kissed her goodbye last time kiss her hello this time. If you didn't kiss her goodbye last time for whatever reason but you're having a second date then greet her appropriately hug her and kiss her on the cheek. She clearly has an interest or the two of you wouldn't be there so it's appropriate. This time as I said it should be a bit more interesting even if it's something as simple as playing crazy golf. You like each other's company enough to want to have fun together, that's my aim for the second date now she feels safe and comfortable with me I want her to have fun with me.

Depending on what you're doing, now can be a good time to add a little competition into the mix. She will also learn a lot about you by how competitive you are, in turn you'll also learn a lot about her by how competitive she is. It can be a good thing if done right, it can be a bad thing if done wrong. I'm talking fun friendly competition in the right setting that you'll both enjoy, so listen carefully. Don't take it too seriously, don't get angry or lose your temper, don't lose on purpose, don't be a sore loser, don't try and make a competition out of something stupid. Make a harmless bet on it if you like (a harmless bet is not a blowjob in the toilets if you win. Think more If I win you buy the drinks after).

For this example let's say you've gone bowling. So a bit of back and forth humour between you two about who's going to win, or teasing if one of you gutters it is good. Staring her down at the beginning and telling her you bet she's shit and you're going to fucking destroy her, not so good. That would not be fun friendly competition for you both to enjoy.


- Don't take it too seriously. You're there to have fun and this is a date. You're there to have fun with your date, don't lose sight of that. If you get a strike smile, if you miss completely laugh. Don't try and turn into a professional bowler all of a sudden it's a date not a league. She wants to know you two are there together, not you're there bowling and she came along.

- Don't get angry. If you gutter it laugh, if you slip over laugh, if you miss the spare don't sulk or lose your shit. If you gutter it, swear and then kick the chair in frustration what do you think is going through her head? Best case scenario, "What a baby." Worst case scenario, "Fuck this, if that's what he's like over bowling what is he going to be like with me when we argue?" (If I've just described your behaviour perfectly in this scenario. You have anger issues and you need to get that sorted before you consider dating.)

- Don't lose on purpose. Don't lose on purpose thinking it will make her like you more or get her approval it won't. She's looking for a man not a doormat. I know as a young child this was something I was told to do by adults and it gets ingrained into some of us. Being told by your parents to let your little sister win the next game, or a teacher telling the boys to let the girls score the next point in PE at primary school gets absorbed into our young minds, it can be hard to shake. Let me tell you fuck that! It's the 21st century and equality has come a long way. If you lose on purpose she won't think you're a gentleman. You'll come across as weak and desperately trying to seek her approval. She knows you're doing it and it won't impress her. If she wants you to lose on purpose so she can win she is either testing you to see if you'll do it, at which point don't be weak it's a test, or she wants you to lose on purpose because she can't stand to lose. That would suggest she's been very spoilt and made to believe she's special without earning it. Probably not a good dating prospect. If you get that impression of her don't lose and see how she reacts.

- Don't be a sore loser. If she kicks your arse she kicks your arse get over it. Again don't sulk it is not attractive. It was supposed to be fun being a sore loser will ruin that and again that's the part of the date she will remember. Later on she will be telling her friends, "yeah it was going well until he sulked the rest of the evening so I came home." It was fun laugh about it.

- Don't try and make a competition out of something stupid. Who gets the highest score you can make a competition out of? That's fine, don't then turn to her and say I bet I can drink my drink faster than you can. Because she's going to think you're a child. So competition if appropriate. Say you'd gone to an art gallery instead competition is not appropriate, you wouldn't walk through the gallery together then suddenly say I'll race you to that painting at the end and take off running. She will think she's gone out with a five-year-old.

Competition if done right is a good thing. She will learn a lot about you, competitiveness can be an attractive quality in a man it can also be an ugly one if done wrong. Moral of the story, show her you have a bit of competitiveness don't show her you're mentally unhinged by it. Finally it's still a date! The point of this was to make it more fun and get to know each other better. I said a bit of competition, it still needs to stay and the date should not become a competition. She is still the woman you're seeing not your rival all of a sudden. You should still be talking, flirting, and getting to know one another this goes for whatever you do.

## Fitting in more than one thing

While it's still important to know when to call it a night and not let it drag on too long. (Remember leave them wanting more) The second date is a good time to consider doing the multiple mini dates in one that I touched on in Chapter six. It's really not difficult. Say you've finished bowling, ask her if she's hungry, say let's get something to eat. I'm sure you don't want chicken nuggets from the attached kitchen so head out the bowling alley into town and find somewhere that looks good. Get a drink after, then walk around the town (if it's not a dump) find somewhere else interesting to get another drink. It's better if you can think a little more outside the box and surprise her a little. "Hey, it's a nice day and the beach is only 30 minutes down the road shall we go for fish and chips?" This can be applied to anything you do if you give it a little thought. If you've done something you both love for your second date this should come even easier to you. let me give you an example other than bowling.

My top second date of all time was a very simple one. Me, her, our dogs, walking boots, a picnic, and the open countryside. Now I got extremely lucky here because I had met someone who was into the same things as me, the outdoors, animals and history. I had been exploring old maps and discovered forgotten ruins from World War Two. I wanted to go and find them. When she heard my plans she wanted to come along. We were both in our element, that meant we were both extremely relaxed around one another meaning everything else that day fell into place without us trying. I'm competent outdoors and I love dogs, so I was naturally confident and leading the way which meant I was presenting her the best version of myself and impressing her without trying to impress her. When we found the ruins we were both equally interested in them. In all we were out for almost nine hours. We had hiked out, found the first thing I wanted to find, stopped for a snack then carried on to the next set of ruins where we had lunch. We now had a long walk back. As we sat there I said to her, "Do you know what I could really go for?" When she asked what I said, "Dessert and maybe something to drink other than water," I said holding up my near empty water bottle. She agreed saying something like, "If only." At which point I showed her the map, "Dog friendly pub just over a mile northeast. What do you think, sticky toffee pudding or the brownie?" We were off and by the time we had done dessert and a drink it was going to be a long walk back to our starting point. There was no way we would make it back before dark. So we got a cab back to the starting point. From there we went to a different pub had another drink and got dinner before she returned home to put her exhausted dog to bed. I never planned for the date to go on for nine hours nor did she. While I knew we wouldn't be far from the first pub once we got to the WW2 ruins, I never planned to have dinner with her that night. It all worked out because we had clicked so well having fun doing something we both really enjoyed. Nothing was forced it all came very naturally.

So if you're doing something you both enjoy it should come easier for both of you. Also on a side note for those of you I addressed in chapter one about being out of touch, there is your proof that you'll find someone who will like the things you like even if they're a little obscure. We literally had the best day, I know a lot of you will be thinking walking miles into the arse end of nowhere to eat a sandwich and look at the remains of something long gone sound boring as shit to me. Fair enough but I found someone who enjoyed it as much as I did.

## After the second date

Once the second date is over if all went well if you didn't kiss goodbye on the first you should kiss her goodbye on the second, assuming you two haven't kissed at some point during the date because the moment was there. If there isn't a kiss by this point your date is either ultra-shy, ultra-religious or you're headed into the friend zone. Same guidelines as for after date one. Go home relax, see some friends, live your life. Don't chase after her right away. Guidelines for setting up your third date are the same as for setting up the second.

The third date and fourth and fifth and sixth and onward really shouldn't be any different from the planning for the second date. The idea is to meet up and have fun together. It really is that simple. Meet up, have fun and have intimacy grow between you Whether you're sky diving, or going to IKEA, meet up, have fun and grow intimacy. Your success in doing that will be greatly helped if you are relaxed, and continue to behave like the strong secure confident man you should be.

# CHAPTER 9

# The silly little mistakes

You're actively dating someone, or dating a few people there are still lots of errors men make and most the time we don't even realise what we're doing. Things that seem very minor to us but can stop any budding relationship from blossoming. If you're doing well so far you want to keep it that way so avoid making these mistakes.

## Don't get caught up with someone you're not interested in

The whole time you're dating, meeting up and having fun, make sure you're having fun, not just making sure she is. The moment you realise you're not having fun you need to take some time and give it some thought. Are you into her, or have you just been going through the motions? No sense in lying to her or yourself. If you're not that into her you need to be honest and not just keep going on with it.

## Don't stop doing things for you

You're dating, granted that takes up some of your time, but you still need to be true to yourself, your life, your goals and make time for yourself. Don't stop doing the things you love, don't stop constantly trying to be the best version of you that you can be. So you've met a girl that doesn't mean screw the diet or quit the gym. It doesn't mean spend less time studying to spend more time with her. She was attracted to you for you. If you stop doing the things that make you who you are what happens? That attraction starts to diminish. Like I said we get complacent, we get sloppy, don't let this happen. If you got in shape while single don't let it all go just because you've started dating someone new. If you overhauled your wardrobe before you started dating don't get lazy and revert back. I know not every date will be a night on the town, some evenings you'll just have her round for dinner or vice versa but there is a middle ground between night on the town and complete slob, find it. I know because I've fallen into this trap before, I'm single living an active happy full life. I meet someone and before you know it all you two do is sit on the couch together in old tracksuits, both of you wondering what has happened? When did you both stop doing the things you loved and how did you become so boring together? This isn't good for either of you don't fall into it.

## Don't stop being a man

The strong confident secure man, can't just be an act at the beginning to impress them, you need to be that man end of story. Don't suddenly become weak, insecure or needy. Don't do stupid things like rush to put a label on it. If things are going well let them keep going well don't all of a sudden be desperate to call her your girlfriend wrap it up and make it official. Don't start calling and texting her all the time, yes communication will increase of course. But you need to remain a man not become someone weak and needy who's in need of constant attention and validation. Trust me if you start chasing or over pursuing them they will run.

Don't become too available. Especially not in the early stages. If you're constantly available do you know what happens? She will become bored of you quickly. Their still needs to be some anticipation some mystery. If she knows you're free at six every night once you've finished work and you'll come over every time, there's not much fun in that is there. Early stages especially she should wonder what you're doing tonight? Hoping you're going to get in contact and ask her out.

Being a man also mean's not becoming her servant or a doormat. Don't start doing things just to seek her approval, don't remain at her beck and call and most important of all don't be afraid of the word NO! Some women know this, other's don't, but they all want a man who isn't afraid to stand up to them. When they're being unreasonable you need to be able to call them on it, believe it or not women need a man who isn't afraid to put them in their place when they are acting out.

Standing up to women has always been my biggest failure. Read and re read this next bit very carefully because this is my hardest learnt lesson. I've spent half my life afraid to disappoint or upset women. This means in the past I've bent over backwards to try and please them when I should have said no. When they've acted out instead of calling them on it I've tried harder and been even nicer to them. The bitchier they got the nicer I became, this lead to them becoming even bitchier, me trying even harder to be nice and them becoming worse. This would go on until it hit rock bottom and they lost all respect for me. At this point they no longer see me as a man, were both miserable and then I'd get dumped.

Does the above sound familiar to you? For years it

was a mystery to me I just didn't understand it. Why had her attraction dropped? Why was she being horrible? Why was me trying harder and making an effort to be extra nice making it worse? The answer has been staring all of us in the face. You stopped being a man in her eyes and she stopped respecting you. Then our solution made it even worse because our response was the behaviour of a weak man who doesn't deserve respect! If you still don't believe me look at it from a different perspective. By being extra nice you're rewarding shitty behaviour. In turn she behaves even worse and you then reward her for it even more. When you had a tantrum as a child did your parents reward you for it, or did they make you regret your decision?

If you can't stand up for yourself why should she respect or want to be with you? If you're getting pushed around by her and she's walking all over you what does it tell her about you? It tells her if you two are out one night and some drunken arsehole is bothering her, won't leave her alone and tries to grab her tits you will be useless! You won't stand up to her how can she believe you will protect her from men like him? If you can't show her your backbone how is she supposed to introduce you to her father? She needs to be confident he's going to look you in the eye shake your hand and think, "yeah my baby girl has found a decent one."

Simple fact is she can't. Understand this is a primal instinct for her. Sure the world has changed, we have evolved. Were no longer cavemen and she doesn't need you to fight off sabre-tooth tigers with a pointy stick but evolution has programmed her to still find a man that can.

This is one of the reason's women go for the "bad boy" and can't seem to leave controlling or abusive men. Despite these men being the biggest arseholes on the planet they're not afraid to say no or put a women in her place. Sadly far too many women mistake abusive or controlling behaviour as strength and put up with it. When really they should see a controlling or abusive man for what he is. Someone who behaves that way because he is in fact incredibly weak inside. I'm not saying don't be nice! You should be nice, I'm definitely not telling you to be controlling or abusive. Just remember you were born with a backbone, don't be afraid to use it. Don't be afraid to disappoint her if necessary, approval seeking behaviour never leads anywhere good. Never be afraid to stand up to anyone if they're out of line. She may not like it in the short term but in the long term it will pay off.

I can't really give you many good examples of this. As I've already admitted standing up to women is probably my biggest failing. It's where many relationships have gone wrong for me. But I do remember one example where I did get it right. Remember the Arrogant Elitist PA I mentioned in Chapter two? We had been to the cinema and were having dinner after. The waiter made a mistake and she had no problem expressing her displeasure at him. After he had left she continued to go on about it. I let this continue for about a minute by then I had truly had enough of her. I stopped her mid-sentence and said, "enough! He made a mistake he's going to fix it, now leave it he's only a kid." She started to protest and I cut her off again. I explained to her that I wanted to have a nice dinner with my girlfriend and enjoy myself. I wasn't going to be able to enjoy myself if she was determined to ruin it by showing her ugly side. I'm not usually like this. It was very out of character for me but she had really rubbed me up the wrong way. Anyway it had a profound effect on her because I couldn't remember the last time she had treated me so well before that. That was what she needed bringing back down to earth.

On a side note Being a man also means standing up for the woman you're with. Even if she's clearly the one in the wrong. Even when she knows she's clearly the one in the wrong as well. So in the example I just gave If the waiter hadn't been a nervous teenager but instead had been someone who would have called her out for being a shitty customer I would have failed at being a man in her eyes if I hadn't stood up for her as well even though she was clearly being a bitch to him. They need to know you'll stand up for them otherwise they won't see you as a man.

## Don't start demanding all of her time

As things progress yes you should be seeing more of each other and at a greater frequency. Let nature take its course. Demanding to much of her time is needy and you can still chase her off. Remember that amazing life you were leading when single? The one that helped attract her to you in the first place. Well if you're suddenly demanding all her time that life was a lie wasn't it? Were you lying to her all along? As much as you still need time for you, she still needs time for herself too. If you start trying to demand to much of each other's time seeing each other starts to become hard work. Hard work does not translate into meet up and have fun does it.

## Sex

When does it happen? Simple answer when both of you want it to. Ignore what movies and TV shows have told you about sex happening on the third date. There is no law, there is no rule. Sex will happen between the two of you when the time is right for the two of you. Some women will be very keen and it will happen early, some may be very cautious. The fact is you don't know her past. She might be very wary as men have previously promised her the world only to disappear once they've slept with her. She might have been sexually harassed or assaulted in the past, you just don't know. One thing I can tell you though is if she's not ready yet, pushing for it will not help! She will think you're just like other arsehole who has mislead her. I've had sex on the first date, the second, the third, the twentieth! It happens when the time is right for the two of you. Of course you need to let her know your intentions and that you're ready for it, but guess what she knows you're a man so it's kind of a given. Kiss her, touch her, see how far it goes but make sure she is comfortable with it. The moment she is not comfortable you stop. If she feels pressured it won't happen again and the one time it does happen won't be a good experience.

## Becoming too serious too soon

As I've said earlier men are more visual, we see

something we like and we focus in on it. Women take a little longer to open up. They need to be stimulated on the emotional level as well as the physical one. Don't be desperate to make her your girlfriend. Just focus on having a good time and making sure you're both enjoying yourselves. Don't start asking questions like, "what are we?" Or "Are you my girlfriend or not?" Remain the strong confident man. When it's time for commitment she will let you know. She will find subtle ways to let you know what she wants if you push the issue you'll be coming across needy and chase her off.

## Don't become predictable or boring

Dating should never stop. Whether you're now in a committed relationship or even married it should never stop. What I said earlier this chapter about finding yourselves never doing anything. Just sat on the couch together in lazy clothes, don't let that happen. You've got to keep things alive and interesting. It's not all that difficult leave the house once in a while. Don't go to the same pub together on the same night at the same time every time. You've got the internet use it. Search "upcoming events near me" I recently discovered the local horse racing track also acts as a drive-in cinema, and open-air concert arena, does casino nights and other themed evenings. Mix things up a bit, it doesn't have to cost you the earth either. Go to town when it's market day, go to the river when there's a sailing event. Even something as simple as finding a new recipe and having something entirely different for dinner once in a while. Like I said you've got the internet use it, everything you need is at your fingertips. Subscribe to one of those websites that offers last minute deals on weekends away at B&B's. Be spontaneous once in a while catch her by surprise. Don't ask shall we do something this weekend? On Friday afternoon tell her she has 30 minutes to pack a bag and be in your car. Don't tell her where you're going just tell her she will need this, this and this.

## Jealousy

It's not an attractive trait on anyone but we all possess it within us to some extent. Most women like a little bit of jealousy it makes them feel desired. It also gives them a weapon when you piss them off! Don't like or trust that guy in her office? Fuck her off and you'll get a text saying she will be a little late tonight they're going for a drink after work. Control your jealousy don't let it show. Jealousy is the sign of a distrustful insecure man. If you're showing it that much about that guy in her office it makes you look weak because clearly you're seeing him as a threat. At the same time this will make her look at him and think hmm what does he see in him that I don't? It's a sad state of affairs that I even need to write this next part but I have seen it before. Being jealous of the love and time a woman gives to her children or pets is ludicrous! If this describes you, seek help.

Never and I mean NEVER expect a woman to put you before her children. If you meet one that does I'd be very cautious something isn't quite right there. If you are dating a woman with children sometimes things won't go to plan, babysitters will cancel or the ex will let her down and not be able to take their kids that evening. It happens, being jealous that the kids monopolise so much of her time is stupid don't get shitty about it. As and when it happens be cool about it. If she can't see you one night because of it find something else to do with your time. Don't let that one moment ruin all future moments. If you're getting jealous over how much she loves a dog or a cat take a step back and take a long hard look at everything because you're being ridiculous.

## Paranoia

Similar to jealousy in some ways but not always founded. If you're paranoid she's going to leave you then it's likely to reflect in your behaviour and cause her to probably do just that. Men who are paranoid their girlfriends will leave them usually act needy, and try to please too much. She will notice your behaviour becoming strange and different and it will probably push her away. on the polar opposite some men will attempt to become overly dominant and controlling if they fear this will happen. They will start doing things like trying to control who she can see and where she can go because they're afraid they might meet someone else or her friends will talk her into seeing sense and leaving them. Newsflash; if this is you you're behaving like an arsehole and she probably should leave you.

Paranoid she will cheat or she is cheating. If you're having this problem you need to look at the root cause and figure out why you're thinking like you are. The two most likely scenarios are you've been cheated on in the past or you're dating someone who has a history of it. First of all I know it sucks. I've been cheated on, it did not bring out the best in me and it took me some time to get over it. But I did get over it. That's the difference You can't assume because one woman did you wrong all the others will as well. If you've now met a decent woman but you're paranoid she will cheat, your thoughts and behaviour is going to be very insulting to her. She shouldn't have to put up with it. Guess what it's likely to push her away Why should she put up with your paranoia when she's done nothing to deserve it? If you're paranoid because you know she has cheated on others in the past you need to make a decision. If you're unwilling to leave her you need to give her the benefit of the doubt because you can't have a relationship like that. If you can't give her the benefit of the doubt then clearly a functional relationship will not be possible between you two and you need to walk away.

Let me make one thing perfectly clear while your actions and behaviour may delay someone from cheating. Whether that's being such an awesome boyfriend they have no desire to seek out someone else, or being so controlling they don't get a chance to seek out someone else. You cannot stop someone from doing it. At the end of the day if someone wants to cheat they will cheat. It's down to them you may be able to delay it but you'll never stop it. If you're exhibiting paranoid behaviour about it, your also showing weak behaviour and that may encourage some women to cheat because weak doesn't do it for them.

Unless you're a secret agent or a mafia boss hiding under a fake identity leave paranoia alone it won't do you any good.

## Don't take her for granted

This can be a fine line to walk. Don't take anyone for granted don't ever stop making them feel desired or special. However you still need to be a man not a doormat don't put her on a pedestal, kiss her feet and worship the ground she walks on. You need to be able to let her know she's desired and special without appearing week or just saying things for her approval. In all it's not too difficult. Listen to her and pay attention. When she's gone and got her hair or her nails done, don't fail to notice. If she's gone clothes shopping and shows you her new dress don't just say, "It's very nice" Tell her that you're not cooking tonight because you two are going out for dinner and she needs to be wearing that dress. It's not rocket science. Don't just compliment her endlessly otherwise your words will mean nothing, soon enough you need to make them count. Don't fail to notice when she does things.

## Sending/receiving nudes and dirty pictures

If you're older than me, this may well be a very new concept to you, if you're younger than me there is a good chance you've already sent and received more than I will in my lifetime. Like all things there is a right way to go about it and a very wrong way to go about it. If you are both into it then it can be fun, exciting, erotic and lead on to great things. If either of you are not into it then it can fuck things up.

The attached stigma. If you're incredibly conservative or you were already an adult long before camera phones were a thing, you may be of the opinion that this is the behaviour of a slut. However it is now a fairly common interaction between couples and consenting individuals. As I've said earlier in this book you can't stop progress even when progress looks strange to you. You may not be into receiving these photos from someone you're dating but do not put down or attempt to slut shame someone if they have enjoyed doing this with someone else in the past or you know they have taken nude photos of themselves. The world is changing we live in the 21st century. Recent years have done a lot for female empowerment, confidence and body positivity. If you've met a woman able to embrace that don't you dare try and tear her down for it you have no right.

I've had exs and female friends with albums of nudes they've taken on their phones. They've taken them for themselves not anyone else. Sometimes a woman just wants to feel sexy, feel empowered and this is one way that some women do this. I have another friend that shares nudes with another friend of hers. Neither of them are gay nor bisexual it's just a ritual they have developed. When one of them has a big day ahead, an important meeting she might send the other one a photo first. It's her way of feeling strong, empowered and confident before doing what she's got to do. So in conclusion if you're not into it you're not into it, that's fine no one can force you but break any stigma you may have about it. It's her body she has every right to be proud of it and enjoy it how she wants. It doesn't just mean she's a slut!

The rules I set in sending your first message still very much apply here, dirty pictures are not an opening asking for or sending. Sharing photo's like this can happen before you meet with someone it can happen after, it might not happen at all. But it is not an opening statement. The first thing you need to understand is the difference in how men and women think when it comes to receiving a nude or risqué picture. As a man, if a woman I was dating or talking to send me an unsolicited nude photo, I generally liked it. It was exciting, it was a turn on. I had a girl once who would sometimes wake up and send me photos of her in bed. It was a huge turn on knowing she had woken up and was thinking of me. I imagine most men are much the same, it was always a nice surprise. Now understand women don't think like us. I'm yet to meet a woman who has told me that receiving an unsolicited nude or dick pic was a turn on. It is usually an instant block or ghosting. Doing this is telling her you only want one thing and that you are like every other "fuckboy" she's rejected. the only time you can get away with this is if you're in a committed relationship with someone and you're both into it. Unsolicited nudes or dick pics in the talking or dating phase are a NO!

*"Fuckboy someone who is only looking for a piece of ass to use then throw away."* – Urban dictionary

Asking for nudes. It's very simple DO NOT DO IT! Again it says you only want one thing and it screams, "I'm a fuckboy". Understand that for a woman to send you a nude she has to feel comfortable enough. She is putting a level of trust in you by doing so. Asking or demanding photo's does not make her feel comfortable or inspire trust.

Below is a word-for-word text conversation with a friend of mine when I told her about writing this book.

*Her* – Did I tell you that a guy asked me to send him nudes for "points" which would be added up and then however many points I got would be what date we went on?

*Me* – You're fucking shitting me! So what did you say to this guy?

*Her* – Told him to fuck off.

**I'll give him credit for original thinking, but don't be like him! Don't be one of those guys.**

So how do you get them? It's a process, whatever you do don't message her saying, "Send nudes," it's been done to death. It's not even funny in an ironic way anymore. You can't just let her know you want nudes you have to make her want to send them. How have I gone about this in the past? Well it's quite simple I've said the right things to make her feel beautiful, make her feel sexy, turn her on and make her know I desire her right then in that exact moment. Pick your moment and seize it. If she's in the mood there will probably be hints in her texts. Pick up on them respond in kind and make her feel good. For example if she's text you saying she's just got home and has been out underwear shopping, she's telling you because she wants you to know. Most women like taking photos of themselves. If you're dating a woman and she's getting dolled up for a night out there's a good chance she'll send you a selfie. It's because she wants to be appreciated. So appreciate her go on from there.

Sending her a dirty picture. well there are two conditions that need to be met. 1.) Does she want you to? 2.) Do you want to? If those two conditions are met then go for it. Things work both ways here, just as I've told you not to pressure a woman into it don't let yourself be pressured into it either. If you don't want to send nude photos don't do it plain and simple. A final point to remember is once that photo is sent it's no longer yours. I've always considered this a bit of a double standard, if a man shows his friends nudes he's received he is an arsehole. Yet women sharing what they've been sent with there's is a given. Odds are her friends will see it if you're not OK with that don't do it.

Another thing to consider. If you're sending nudes to someone you haven't met yet. How sure are you that you're talking to who you think you are?

## NAVIGATING THE MINEFIELD

What's the worst case scenario? What if you're being cat-fished by someone who's underage? You could be entering some very murky waters I'm not sure how good a legal defence ignorance is.

If you're receiving or have received nudes. It's very simple if you like it let them know you appreciate it, but be original, the winky face emoji just isn't going to cut it. If you're confident enough respond in kind. Don't just respond with a dick pic though (It's probably not what they want to see) plus I said be original. The top three responses I have ever given according to women are. When in return I sent a video of my hand grabbing the bed sheet and clenching it into a fist. When she knew I was at work so I replied with a video of me going wide eyed and "Accidentally" dropping my phone under the desk. I have my tongue pierced so another time I responded to a nude with a GIF of me rolling my tongue bar across my upper lip. Be original think outside the box. To most women taking a nude is an art form. They've taken angles and lighting into account, the photo you've received is probably the 30th one she took before she was happy with it. So you've got to show your appreciation, as men we really can't do sexy like a woman can. So that's why my photo or video responses are usually me showing appreciation rather than trying to respond exactly in kind. If you're not confident enough to respond exactly in kind think of something better to say than just "wow" but take a hint. She's not sending you things like this just for you to say "very nice" get the confidence to respond in kind remember what I said about confidence being attractive. Most men will reply with just a "wow" and an emoji be different.

Think of it this way, I said earlier we were the more visual of the sexes. That's why men go for the magazines on the top shelf and women go for the love story. We want to see it, they want the fantasy. Badly written novels about a tall mysterious gardener in the chateau. This is why you need to build them into it, to put them in the mood in the first place. If you succeed this is why they don't just want a picture of what's between your legs in response. It's also why, "wow very nice" isn't going to cut it either. I don't know if you've ever read a woman's romance novel but trust me the point in the book where the woman is finally alone with the tall mysterious gardener doesn't end with him saying, "wow nice rack." Make her feel good make her feel desired let her know you wish you were there right now, make her wish you were there too. Tell her what she wants to hear.

A final point on receiving nudes, don't come to expect it. As men it's a given that we are always up for it. Women's moods change they ebb and flow.

Just because she was in the mood one day and was sending you nudes it doesn't mean she will be the same tomorrow or the rest of the week. If you've come to expect it, then don't get it, you might do something stupid like demand it, then you've probably fucked it.

## Learning the difference between what a woman says versus what she really means

I wish I could write a literal translation dictionary for this because if I had the knowledge to do it I would be a multimillionaire. Sadly while I have got a lot better than when I started I still speak female at a novice level. While we use the same alphabet and the same words, men and women communicate using two very different translations of the English language. I touched on this a little earlier with the example of realising my then girlfriend was not over her ex. Sometimes her words are not going to line up with her moods, actions or behaviour. You won't understand, it's because you haven't learnt how to decode and decipher what she's saying. If you're not following so far I'll give you the classic example every man has had. "I'm fine!" Or, "it's fine!" We've all heard that one haven't we gents? We all knew whatever it was it was far from fine as well didn't we! Years ago I adopted a fuck it attitude towards this. I would say. "OK" and carry on as normal doing whatever I wanted. I thought to myself (In some cases even said it to girlfriends faces) If you can't talk to me like an adult, use your big girl words and drop this passive aggressive bullshit then it's your problem not mine. I wish I could tell you that it worked. I was very wrong. While in some circumstances this approach did get them to communicate it came with a lot more venom and sting because of it.

Again you might find the thought of this incredibly annoying and think like I did back in the day, why can't they just tell it like it is? It would be so much easier. While true first off, were not exactly innocent of it ourselves are we guys? When she wants to wear that dress you hate because it makes her look like her mother crossed with a zoo creature have you said it like that to her outright or have you taken a more subtle approach? Women are not all that different in how they communicate to us at times. The blame for this falls on us as well. Our behaviour is part of the reason they won't be blunt and to the point with us.

Ever approached a woman only to be rejected by her telling you she has a boyfriend? Maybe she did but the odds are she didn't, she just wasn't interested in you. This is something that was bought to my attention on a feminist Instagram page. A woman complained, "Why is it safer for me to tell a guy I have a boyfriend instead of no thank you or I'm not interested?" It really got me thinking because as a man I had never looked at it like that before, why would I? So here it is. That woman won't tell a guy in a bar who's a complete stranger, "No thanks." Because she doesn't know how he will react or what he will do. Best case scenario he will say, "OK fair enough well have a nice evening." Worst case scenario he's an aggressive arsehole with a fragile ego she's just bruised and won't take no for an answer. Women have learnt that if they reject guys like this they're likely to face a barrage of abuse. "What do you mean no? Why not? What's wrong me with? You think you're too good for me? You think I'm ugly? Fuck you bitch I was only being friendly!" No woman wants or deserves this and sadly too many of them have learnt the hard way. So they've learnt to say no without saying no, "Sorry, I have a boyfriend."

This is one of the things I liked about online dating. It was one of the few places a woman had the power to be honest. The internet gave her the safety to just ignore me if she wasn't interested. I preferred that. No reply meant no thanks and I moved on, no wondering if she was just being nice for the sake of it, no wondering if she had given me a fake number or if she had deleted mine as soon as I gave it to her. No wondering if I would actually hear from her or if she was feigning interest because she's been conditioned to not be honest with men.

You will have to learn to speak this language if you want things to progress and become harmonious, at the very least you'll have to recognise when something's been mistranslated. Women will very rarely be blunt and to the point with you whether they don't want to hurt your feelings or they're afraid of the consequences. So they drop odd hints or say something that means something totally different. Ever heard these before, "It's not you it's me," translation it was definitely you. "I'm just not in the right place for this right now," translation you fucked it up dickhead. I covered this a bit in Chapter seven when a girl says I think we should just be friends. It's because she's not going to say. "You were getting there but then you messed up when you said this or did this or failed to do that. Now I don't see you as a strong man and my vagina isn't going to get wet for you" is she? You need to learn how to decode this because this secret language becomes most prevalent when something is wrong. AKA when you've messed up, therefore you need to know so you can fix it.

Another stupid mistake to make when it comes to decoding women is asking them for advice. Of course there are lots of things you should ask them for advice on. Get your female friends to take you clothes shopping, get them to help you pick gifts, or flowers, it makes sense. Asking them for advice because the woman you're dating has started behaving strange not so much. Odds are they won't be completely honest with you either. I can remember a couple of years ago being sat in a beer garden as a friend of mine explained his woes to me and two female friends of his. One I knew, one I had just met. As we listened to him they came out with things like, "I don't know, maybe she's afraid of commitment. I don't know what her problem is you were perfect, I wish a guy would do that for me." Once they were done coddling him. I looked him in the eye and said, "Ignore everything they've just said they are afraid of hurting your feelings, the fact is when you did this you fucked it, when you said that you fucked it and when you tried to fix it by doing that you proper fucked it. You turned her off and now she just isn't interested in you romantically." I got two very dirty looks and a tongue lashing from the both of them for accusing them of being liars or wrong. But a little later as my friend went in the pub to get the next round I turned to them both and said, "Be honest he can't hear us. If you were that girl, you were with him and he did that would the outcome be any different?" Neither of them denied it.

I had the same thing happen to me before as well. In my early 20's I remember going up to Northampton to spend the weekend with my girlfriend who was there in university. I hadn't seen her for a while and pulled out all the stops. I thought I was perfect, romantic and had blown her away all weekend. Unbeknown to me at the time I had made some fuck ups that would be obvious to me now and our relationship ended not long after. I remember spilling my guts to a female friend of mine down the phone who was up at the University of Manchester. Again she assured me it was my ex not me. She was lucky to have me! She would regret breaking up with me. She wished a guy would do that for her she would have loved everything I did. Well a couple of months later her boyfriend went up to visit her. He had the same thoughts as me evidently and gave her the weekend she told me she wished a guy would give her. A week later she was on the phone to me moaning about how she had to dump him after he came up to see her for the weekend. I remember being on the phone thinking hold on I'm having serious déjà vu.

Final point to make on this when I wrote the part in Chapter six about showing up with flowers or gifts. I asked my wife her opinion. I asked if anyone had ever done it before she met me. She said, "No but it would have been nice." I asked several friends and I got a couple of similar responses a couple of women I know said they think they would have liked it if a guy had done that. After I had finished writing that section I then text it to every woman who said that and showed my writing to my wife. After thinking on it they all agreed with me. If a guy had shown up with flowers it would not have done him any favours. Sometimes women say or think they want something but it's far from the truth. A bit like how many women think they'd love a nice guy who'd do anything for them when the truth is they need and want a guy who will stand up to them.

## Failing to open up, opening up too soon or too much

Throughout this book I've told you not to give out your life story. I've said you should have a bit of mystery about you. I standby these statements 100%, as you are dating someone you should ask more questions about her than tell her about yourself. She should want to know about you and she should find things out by asking, not by having you tell her unprompted. Think back to what I touched on earlier when I said men go for the dirty magazines and women go for the love story. If you tell her everything about you and lay it all out there right away you're giving her the dirty magazine there's nothing left for the imagination. Women want the love story they want the fantasy. By having a bit of mystery and not telling her everything you're giving her that love story, as she asks and learns about you piece by piece that's the story line unfolding.

This has to be done correctly, I'm not saying don't open up to her at all if you remain a closed book it won't work. She will think you're either a robot devoid of life and personality or you're hiding something. If you open up to soon the story is over. Imagine this is a romance novel and you're the fantasy the story line is pushing. Opening up to soon and telling her everything is the same as giving away the ending of that book before she got to the big love scene in the middle. Most women want that love story, they want to figure it out themselves and have it unfold. Let them!

Don't open up to much, by this I mean don't be too eager to drag the skeletons out of the closet first chance you get. To many people do this, they take all their dark secrets, the ugly parts of their past and lay them on the table. Don't do it, especially not in the dating phase remember what I said about avoiding negativity, opening up is one thing but keep the dungeon of horrors locked for the time being. Someone you're dating doesn't need to know about any childhood trauma or monumental disasters you've suffered from. You're dating looking for a girlfriend not a therapist. Same goes if you've had a really shitty day don't go on a date and unload on them it will put her off. If you've got to unload see your mates for a few drinks instead. Sure as things progress from dating and you find yourself in a relationship things will go further you'll look to each other for emotional support, you'll learn each other's secrets. She is still your girlfriend though not your mate, not your therapist. She wants you to be her boyfriend not a weak whiny little bitch of a man who comes home and cries in her arms all the time.

Say you've had a really shit day at work. By all means when you see her tell her you haven't had a good day and talk about it. Know the difference between talking to her and talking to your mates about it though. She doesn't need to hear you call your boss every insult you can think of or hear how you want to kick him down the fire escape then beat him to death with his own briefcase. If you want to talk like that go to the pub and do it in the company of your friends. If you've suffered some raw emotional trauma in the past that can only be described in a psychologists office using dolls, then seek professional help do not drop it on her every time it rears its ugly head. Once in a committed relationship she may want to know about it and you can tell her. A decent woman will want to support you and be there for you. But she is not your therapist and should not be treated as such. There is only so much of this someone can take, after that they'll leave.

## Falling down at the first hurdle

The biggest mistake most men make. You are going to fall down, you need to get back up! You need to keep getting back up every time. Dating can be a sprint, it can be a marathon, you might have success early you might not. You might have initial success then go through a long dry spot, too many people who try it give up long before they reach the finish line. You're most likely going to have some bad dates, at some point you'll get rejected, it doesn't mean it's over it doesn't mean give up. You have to pick yourself up and keep going until you find what you want. Most things worth having don't come easy, and life doesn't reward a quitter.

# IN CONCLUSION

If you got this far let me start off by thanking you, the reader. I hope this material proves worth your time and you are able to put it to good use in the future. As I said in the very beginning I'm not a pick up artist or an expert in women. Truth be told every time I've started to think I knew what I was doing, someone would come along to prove different. The more I learnt I realised in the grand scheme of things I knew even less than I thought. My one saving grace is that I've never wanted to stop learning. Just like an athlete needs to constantly practice and train. You should be no different when it comes to life and love. You should constantly want to learn and be better.

That is how I found success with women leading to where I am now. I never gave up I learnt from my mistakes, I knew my limitations and most important of all I sought help in my weakest areas. I found good material and I studied it. I never gave up trying to be the best version of me that I could. The same as you need to study for an exam it never hurts to study for life and love so you can improve yourself live life and love better.

I know in this book I have not gone into great detail about psychology, understanding women, decoding what they say versus what they mean, body language, women testing you, how to pass these tests, wooing, seducing or sex. That's because I know my limitations. I know what I've done wrong in the past I know what's worked for me in the past but I do not consider myself expert enough to give you advice on this and be 100% confident in what I am selling. Instead I am going to move onto the next thing I did right. I sought help.

The best advice I can give you when it comes to better understanding women are names. Corey Wayne and Bruce Bryans. Where my skill set and advice ends These guys are just beginning. You will find Corey Wayne at:

www.understandingrelationships.com

I know if we met in person me and Corey would not get along, we have two very different personality types. However I cannot deny that he really knows what he is talking about, he is far better qualified to guide you in the places I am not. To date he has written two books which you can download for free from his website. I have lost count how many times I've read his books by the way. Whenever I start to feel rusty I pick them right back up. It is also worth subscribing to his video coaching email and his

YouTube channel. He has helped me immensely on more than one occasion. If you have a problem you can email him and he will usually feature you on his YouTube page, anonymously of course.

You'll find Bruce Bryans at:

www.brucebryans.com

Bruce has written an excellent series of books which have helped me grow and increased my understanding astronomically. To date he has six books written for the benefit of men. I cannot recommend them enough. I've downloaded them on audible and often listen to his work while going about my day-to-day tasks.

So what are you waiting for? They're out there, waiting! She's out there somewhere, you just need to find her. Remember to enjoy yourself and have fun every step of the way. Otherwise what's the point? Oh yeah and don't be an arsehole.

Thank you everyone who helped me while I wrote this book. You know who you are! Those of you that offered encouragement. Those of you who shared your horror stories. Those of you that gave up your free time to read through early drafts, call me an idiot and correct my grammar. I never would have finished this without you.

# ABOUT THE AUTHOR

Phil spent most of his twenties solo travelling around the world. To finance this he worked several odd jobs, from security guard, fitness instructor, bouncer, taxicab dispatcher, lifeguard and bartender. This meant that for most of his life at work or travelling he was an outsider looking in, meaning he always got a front row seat to observe the best and the worst of human interaction. Over time he noticed patterns in behaviour as well as the reactions that followed, giving him a unique and somewhat different perspective to the way he saw the world compared to others. This meant friends often came to him to receive different or unusual advice to situations that required out of the box thinking. A term that today his friends refer to as "Sherlocking" it was in one of these "Sherlocking" moments that Navigating the Minefield was born.

Moving back to the UK in 2010 after living in New Zealand Phil now resides in an old pub in a tiny village in rural Wiltshire. He works as a dog handler and as a volunteer on a nature reserve. When not working he usually can't be found as he will be wandering in the middle of nowhere surrounded by dogs. His speciality is finding wilderness areas with no mobile phone signal.

Printed in Dunstable, United Kingdom